The **Institute of Southeast Asian Studies** was established as an autonomous organization in May 1968. It is a regional research centre for scholars and other specialists concerned with modern Southeast Asia, particularly the multi-faceted problems of stability and security, economic development, and political and social change.

The Institute is governed by a twenty-two-member Board of Trustees comprising nominees from the Singapore Government, the National University of Singapore, the various Chambers of Commerce, and professional and civic organizations. A ten-man Executive Committee oversees day-to-day operations; it is chaired by the Director, the Institute's chief academic and administrative officer.

The **Social Issues in Southeast Asia (SISEA)** programme was established at the Institute in 1986. It addresses itself to the study of the nature and dynamics of ethnicity, religions, urbanism, and population change in Southeast Asia. These issues are examined with particular attention to the implications for, and relevance to, an understanding of problems of development and of societal conflict and co-operation. SISEA is guided by a Regional Advisory Board comprising senior scholars from the various Southeast Asian countries. At the Institute, SISEA comes under the overall charge of the Director while its day-to-day running is the responsibility of the Co-ordinator.

Ageing in Asean
ITS SOCIO-ECONOMIC
CONSEQUENCES

CHEN AI JU and GAVIN JONES

In collaboration with

Lita Domingo
Pitchit Pitaktepsombati
Hananto Sigit
Masitah Bte Mohd Yatim

ISEAS Social Issues in Southeast Asia
INSTITUTE OF SOUTHEAST ASIAN STUDIES

Final Inter-Country Report of the ASEAN Ageing Project,
Phase III ASEAN Population Programme.

Published by
Institute of Southeast Asian Studies
Heng Mui Keng Terrace
Pasir Panjang
Singapore 0511

Cataloguing in Publication Data

Chen, Ai Ju.
    Ageing in ASEAN: its socio-economic consequences/Chen Ai Ju and
    Gavin Jones.
    1.   Aged — Employment — ASEAN countries.
    2.   Aged — Medical care — ASEAN countries.
    3.   Aged — ASEAN countries — Social conditions.
    I.   Jones, Gavin W.
    II. Institute of Southeast Asian Studies (Singapore). Social Issues in
        Southeast Asia.
    III. Title.
HQ1064 A9C51   1989   s1s89-66983

ISBN 981-3035-36-6

Typeset by Letraprint

Printed in Singapore by Kin Keong Printing Co. Pte. Ltd.

CONTENTS

LIST OF TABLES

LIST OF FIGURES

ACKNOWLEDGEMENT

The "Socio-Economic Consequences of the Ageing of the Population" project is one of the seven projects of the Phase III ASEAN Population Programme funded by the Government of Australia and co-ordinated by the ASEAN Population Co-ordination Unit.

This report is published by the Institute of Southeast Asian Studies on behalf of the project.

FOREWORD

The "Socio-Economic Consequences of the Ageing of the Population" project is one of the seven population projects of the Phase III ASEAN Population Programme. At the time of its inception, the then five member states of ASEAN — Indonesia, Malaysia, the Philippines, Singapore, and Thailand — agreed to participate in the study under the lead of Singapore. The Project is designed to provide information to policy-makers and planners on the extent of ageing, its implications, and the potential problems which might emerge as a consequence of ageing in each country. It also serves to review the conditions of the aged in different environmental settings and the existing policies and programmes for the elderly in the context of the overall development of the participating countries.

The decision to focus attention on this subject arose out of the realization that the region as a whole is making rapid strides towards completing the demographic transition into a mature society. Presently, the proportion of old persons is still small in ASEAN countries when compared with the West. Therefore, what is faced is not an immediate crisis of ageing but rather a steady trend which will lead to changes in the way societies work.

The political will which inspired the ASEAN Population Programme originated from the ASEAN Summit Meeting in 1976. The Declaration of ASEAN Concord called for the "intensification and expansion of existing co-operation in meeting the problems of population growth in the ASEAN region". Since then a total of nineteen projects under the umbrella of the ASEAN Population Programme have been implemented with the ultimate objective of improving the quality of life in the ASEAN region. The seven projects under the Phase III ASEAN Population Programme were funded by the Government of Australia.

The Project "Socio-Economic Consequences of the Ageing of the Population" was initiated in 1984. It has undertaken a series of activities under its aegis. A review of literature on ageing issues and secondary data analysis provided a springboard for further action. Existing policies and programmes were studied and evaluated, and projections of the aged population made. A survey of the socio-economic profiles of the aged and their attitude towards ageing was carried out in each country with certain core items of information sought so that inter-country comparisons could be made. A study visit was also made to the relevant organizations and facilities in Australia and Japan to examine and observe the policies and programmes for the elderly in these countries. These two countries were identified as they have, among the countries in this region, a relatively larger proportion of elderly and well established programmes for them. These visits enabled the study directors to learn from the experiences of these two countries. Towards the end of the project, national seminars were held in each participating country to discuss with policy-makers and planners the project findings and their implications on the socio-economic development of the country. In these seminars important issues were highlighted and recommendations made.

It is appropriate that the Project culminates with this ASEAN Inter-Country Report to tie together all the knowledge and information gathered over the past years. This report will serve as a useful reference for all concerned with the issues of ageing.

I would like to thank Dr Gavin Jones of the Australian National University, the Project Consultant, and the Country Project Directors — Dr Hananto Sigit, Director of the Bureau of National Accounts, Central Bureau of Statistics, Indonesia; Mrs Masitah Bte Mohd Yatim, Deputy Director of the Division for Population Studies and Evaluation, Population and Family Development Board, Malaysia; Dr Lita Domingo, Associate Professor at the Population Institute, University of the Philippines; and Dr Pitchit Pitaktepsombati, Associate Professor at the School of Public Administration, National Institute of Development Administration, Bangkapi, Thailand — for their hard work and unflagging enthusiasm, and for their contributions to this book. Through their efforts the Project has achieved its main object-ive of raising the awareness of policy-makers and planners to the potential problems which might emerge in the process of ageing in ASEAN.

Dr Chen Ai Ju
Regional Project Co-ordinator
ASEAN Population Project
Socio-Economic Consequences of
the Ageing of the Population.

1
INTRODUCTION

The proportion of old people is still very small in ASEAN countries, when compared with Western countries. In 1980, the proportion of the population aged over 60 was 7.2 per cent in Singapore, 5.7 per cent in Malaysia, and around 5 per cent in Thailand, the Philippines, and Indonesia. In Western countries, by contrast, this proportion ranges between about 12 and 30 per cent. The question might then be raised as to why it is necessary at this time to consider ageing a phenomenon deserving of serious attention in the ASEAN region. The answer is not that an ageing crisis is just around the corner; it is not. By the turn of the century, the proportion of aged in ASEAN countries will still be below 8 per cent, except in Singapore. But in all cases, the proportion will be rising. In other words, the number of old people will be increasing faster than those at all other ages. This trend will continue at an accelerating pace in the early twenty-first century. Therefore, what is faced is not an immediate crisis of ageing, but rather a steady trend which will lead to many changes in the way societies work, and raise many questions about appropriate approaches to problems raised by the steadily increasing share of old people in the population. The time to begin examining these issues is now, not later when the issues have assumed major importance and some of the options may have been foreclosed.

Population ageing over the next decade or two will be of a different order of magnitude in Singapore compared to the other ASEAN countries. Cowgill and Holmes (1970) have proposed that populations should be considered as "aged", "mature", "youthful", and "young" on the basis of the proportion of total population aged 65 and over:

> Less than 4 per cent — young
> 4 to 6 per cent   — youthful
> 7 to 9 per cent   — mature
> 10 per cent and over — aged

Translated into proportions aged 60+ (the measure used in the present study) the definitions would be roughly as follows:

> Less than 6 per cent — young
> 6 to 10 per cent   — youthful
> 11 to 14 per cent   — mature
> 15 per cent and over — aged

According to this definition, Singapore's population is still youthful, though by the year 2000 it will have entered the "mature" bracket and by about the year 2015 — 30 years from now — it will have become aged.[1] It is unlikely that any of the other ASEAN countries will enter the "mature" bracket before the second decade of the twenty-first century, though much depends on the pace of fertility decline over the coming years.

The present report is based on country reports prepared under the Socio-Economic Consequences of the Ageing of the Population Project, a component of the ASEAN Population Project. Preliminary country reports were prepared to summarize what is known about ageing in the region; subsequently a survey of aspects of ageing was conducted in each of the countries. This inter-country report cannot present as much detail on each country as the individual country reports. Rather, it attempts to summarize and synthesize materials presented in more complete form in those reports.

The emphasis in this project has been to consider ageing not as a "problem" but as a phenomenon with positive and negative aspects. The ageing of population is inevitable; it is part and parcel of the attainment of a sustainable demographic balance, at low levels of fertility and mortality. As Notestein (1954) has rightly stated,

> viewed as a whole the 'problem of ageing' is no problem at all. It is only the pessimistic way of looking at a great triumph of civilization.... With a perversity that is strictly human, we insist on con-

sidering the aggregate result of our individual success [at achieving
our goal of individual survival] as a 'problem'.

Issues raised by the ageing of the population have now
become a major preoccupation of governments in Western countries, including Japan. The government of China, too, realizes
that dramatic shifts in age structure will occur if the one-child
family goal is attained. The papers presented at the World
Assembly on Ageing, held in 1982 under the auspices of the
United Nations (U.N.), attest to the thorough research being conducted into all aspects of ageing, including areas such as ageing
and the family, health and recreational needs, employment
problems of the aged, income maintenance, and social service
requirements.

Generational conflicts can arise as the demographic balance
of the population moves in favour of the old; Preston (1984)
argued in his 1984 presidential address to the Population Association of America that people over 65 in the United States had been
relatively advantaged between the 1960s and 1980s in receipt of
publicly supplied goods and services, compared with children.
In large measure this reflected the ability of the older generation to mobilize power through the electoral process, and to apply
pressure on legislators in the form of highly organized lobbying
efforts.

In many parts of ASEAN, it is commonly assumed that the
traditional role of the family in caring for its elderly will avoid
many of the problems faced by Western countries. This may be
true, and it is certainly to be hoped that it is true. But it is by
no means certain. The key question is whether it is "Westerniza-
tion" that leads to increasing unwillingness of families to reside
with and otherwise care for their aged, or whether this phenomenon in the West is a natural outcome of demographic and
economic trends there.

The following appear to be some of the key issues raised by
the rapidly rising number, and less rapidly rising share, of old
people in the region:

1. What will be the effect on dependency ratios and the capacity
   of the economies of the region to sustain the costs associated
   with a growing proportion of aged dependants? As discussed
   in more detail below, the problem here is not so much one

of an increasing absolute dependency burden as it is one of a shift in the main dependant group from the young to the old. There will therefore have to be a corresponding shift in policies and programmes for dependants.

2. To what extent can the traditional veneration of the old, and integration of the old into the three-generation family, be expected to be maintained as the share of the old in the total population increases and families in many cases become four-generation? One point to bear in mind here is that the very forces causing the ageing of the population (that is, the lessened desire for large families due to the increased costs and lowered benefits of children to parents, leading to a decline in fertility) are likely to be associated with a decreased willingness, or at least, availability, on the part of at least some of the young people to care for their parents in old age.

3. What adjustments will be needed in public housing policy in the cities if families are to be encouraged to have elderly parents live with them? Public housing policies geared to a two-child nuclear family normally result in the design of housing units unsuited to a three- or four-generation family.

4. For the increasing proportion of the labour force working in formal sector employment in urban areas, what are the implications of ageing trends for retirement ages and superannuation and pension schemes?

5. What appropriate balance can be struck in the provision of services and income support to the destitute aged between the need to support those who are truly deserving and the need to encourage families to look after their own members to the best of their ability?

6. Given the current rethinking world-wide about appropriate health care systems, what systems will best meet the goals of cost containment, equitable access to health care, and increased involvement of individuals and communities in their own health care, while ensuring that the particular needs of the aged are adequately met?

7. As the number and proportion of old people increase, how can their potential contribution in the work-force, family, and community life be most effectively harnessed?

WHO ARE THE AGED?

It has been noted that the concept of childhood was an invention of eighteenth century Western Europe (Aries 1973). Before that time, children were simply "small adults" who started work at an early age, and were not deemed to require a special status with regular schooling, time for play, need for toys, etc. Similarly, the concept of old age is one that can be defined and redefined for different purposes. In some countries, there is a more precise perception of the age at which old age begins than in others. In Thailand, for example, old age begins at 60. Age is still computed in twelve-year cycles, and the sixtieth birthday marks the completion of the fifth cycle. After reaching this age, a person will be addressed by younger persons with special terms of respect, the equivalents of the kinship terms "grandfather" or "grandmother", even though the speaker may not be related to the older person in any kinship sense at all (Cowgill 1970).

Different concepts about what constitutes old age are no doubt partly responsible for the different ages set for compulsory retirement of civil servants in the ASEAN region, which are: Indonesia — 55 years; Malaysia — 55 years; the Philippines — optional at 60, compulsory at 65; Singapore — 60 years; and Thailand — 60 years. The fact that in Indonesia and Malaysia, the compulsory retirement age for civil servants is set at 55 reflects the accepted belief that by that age, a person in general may no longer be capable of sustained hard work. These beliefs are well grounded in the historical situation in Indonesia and Malaysia: high morbidity associated with the high levels of mortality did take its toll, and few older people were therefore still as strong and active as many of their counterparts in low mortality countries. Conditions change, however. In due course the retirement age in Indonesia and Malaysia may well be raised to 60 years, and the corresponding perception of what constitutes an aged person will alter. It is surprising that even in Singapore, the customary retirement age of 55 (or 60 in the case of public sector employees), which was set years ago when life expectancy was low, still prevails.

For the purposes of this project, it was agreed to consider the population aged 60 years and above as the aged.[2] Therefore in this inter-country report, most of the data presented on the aged will refer to those in this age group. However, because in many comparative studies, the aged are defined as those aged 65 and above, those aged 60–64 will be isolated as a separate subgroup so that the characteristics of the 65+ group can also be studied.

Notes

1. The U.N. (1956) had earlier proposed that populations in which the proportion aged 65 and over exceeded 7 per cent should be considered as "aged". According to this definition, Singapore's population will become aged before the year 2000, or during the next 10 or 15 years.
2. The report of the Secretary General to the U.N.'s World Assembly on Ageing in 1982 stated that it was regrettable to note the recent tendency to regard old age as starting at 60 even though the average life expectancy is increasing and the physical and mental state of sexagenarians in developed countries is superior to what it was 30 or 40 years ago. He also states that "the defining age of 60 is ill adapted to the situation in the developing countries", but fails to give reasons why this is considered to be so. It should be noted that the terms "aged", "elderly", "60+", and "60 and over" are used interchangeably throughout this book.

2
DEMOGRAPHIC BACKGROUND TO THE AGEING PROCESS

The ageing of population is a twentieth century phenomenon, but it is not one that is likely to be reversed. Indeed a historical perspective on world population trends will convince us that the ageing of populations throughout the world is inevitable. It is therefore something to be accommodated and planned for, not to be fought against. Ageing is inevitable simply because of the finite nature of the earth's resources, which implies that continued population growth is not possible.[1] The only civilized way to bring population growth to an end is to balance low mortality rates with low fertility rates: the alternative is high mortality and fertility, the condition prevailing through most of mankind's history. It is a demographic fact of life that populations with low mortality and fertility will, after these trends have been established for some time, have a high proportion of elderly people.

Thus it can be said that the medical and public health advances of the past two centuries have guaranteed that populations will age. This is not so much because people are living longer (though in popular understanding this is often believed to be the main cause of ageing) as because lowered mortality means accelerated rates of population growth (which cannot long be sustained) unless birth rates fall. And it is the fall in birth rates which is the crucial determinant of ageing, through its effect in undercutting the base of the age pyramid (U.N. 1956; Coale 1956).

A few moments' thought should convince the reader that mortality declines in ASEAN countries do not *directly* serve as

a major cause of ageing. Such declines are often heavily concentrated at the infant and childhood ages. As such, their effects are
similar to those of a rise in the birth rate, resulting in more
people at the base of the age pyramid. It is only after mortality
declines have been in progress for a long time that they tend to
be relatively greatest at the older ages, thus reinforcing the
tendency for the population to age.

The importance of declining fertility in the ageing process
can usefully be examined by studying a series of age pyramids
for Singapore (Figure 2.1). In 1957, the Singapore population
had a typical developing country age structure, with a broad-
based age pyramid reflecting the ever-increasing cohorts of
babies being born. A drastic fertility decline after 1957 led to an
undercutting of the base of this pyramid by 1980, whereas the
large "baby boom" cohorts were by this time moving into the
reproductive ages. By the year 2000, the base of the pyramid will
have assumed the more rectangular form typical of low fertility
countries, and the high fertility "bulge" will be in the older
working ages. By the year 2030, the age structure will have
stabilized into the rectangular form of an established low fertility population. The numbers aged 60 and over will have increased enormously compared with 1980, whereas the number
of children will barely have changed over this 50-year period if
fertility remains at the 1985 level.

Singapore's changing age structure is, by ASEAN standards,
an extreme case. Therefore in Figure 2.2 are presented the projected trends in age structure in Thailand according to Thailand's
official low fertility projection. These are more representative
of likely developments in Malaysia and Indonesia as well, if
their recent fertility declines continue. The trend is clearly
towards the Singapore situation, though with a lag of some 20
years and with a less severe undercutting of the base of the age
pyramid. On recent trends, the transformation of the age structure of the Philippines is likely to be lagged even more.

In this report, future ageing prospects in the ASEAN countries will be analyzed based on the latest U.N. projections for each
country (U.N. 1987). In some cases, different fertility and mortality variants will be used to highlight the implications of alternative trends. In all cases, except Singapore,[2] further declines
in both fertility and mortality are assumed, though the speed
of the assumed declines varies.

It should perhaps be stressed that survival rates for the elderly are the least reliable segment of life tables for ASEAN countries, and the projection of these rates is also a very uncertain exercise. Because the levels and trends of these rates directly affect the number and composition of the elderly population in the projections, this uncertainty directly translates into uncertainty regarding the future numbers and age-sex composition of the elderly population. This should be borne in mind, in the discussion that follows.

Table 2.1 shows projected trends in the aged proportion of the population in ASEAN countries from 1980 to 2020. In all cases, the share of the aged is expected to rise by the year 2000, although it will climb still faster beyond that year. It is worth noting that even in the projection for Malaysia, which reflects the government's pro-natalist stance in aiming for a population of 70 million in 115 years, the aged proportion still climbs steadily, reaching 12.6 per cent in the year 2030.

By the year 2025 the proportion of the elderly in the ASEAN countries, with the exception of Singapore, will remain well below its level in Western countries (Table 2.2). However, the levels in the year 2025 in ASEAN countries will be comparable with the levels reached in many Western countries at the pre-

TABLE 2.1
**Projection of Population Aged 65 and Over
in ASEAN and Other Countries**
(In percentages)

	1980	1990	2000	2010	2020
ASEAN					
Indonesia	3.3	3.8	4.9	6.1	7.4
Malaysia	3.7	3.9	4.4	5.6	7.8
Philippines	3.4	3.5	3.8	4.7	6.3
Singapore	4.7	5.6	7.1	9.2	14.5
Thailand	3.5	3.9	4.7	5.7	7.5
OTHER COUNTRIES					
China	4.7	5.9	7.2	8.2	11.4
Hong Kong	6.4	8.4	10.0	10.4	12.1
Japan	9.0	11.4	15.1	18.0	20.8
Republic of Korea	3.8	4.4	5.8	7.6	9.6
Sri Lanka	4.3	5.1	6.4	7.6	10.2

SOURCE: Medium projections, U.N. (1987).

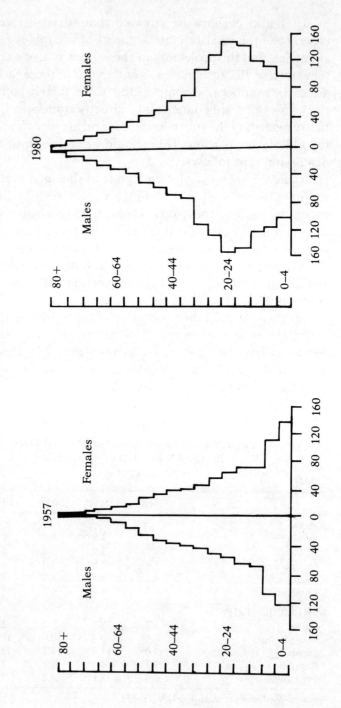

FIGURE 2.1
Age Pyramids 1957 and 1980 and Projected for 2000 and 2030, Singapore
(Number in thousands)

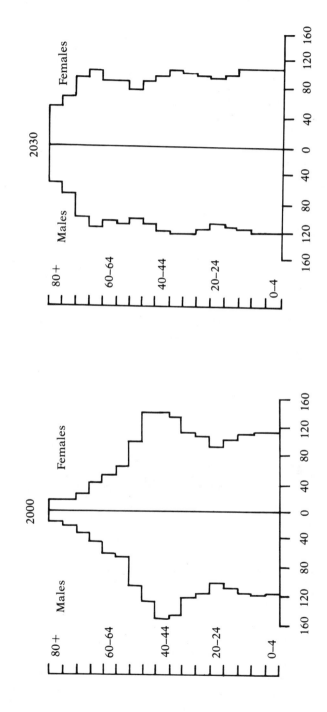

FIGURE 2.1 (Cont'd)

FIGURE 2.2

Age Pyramid 1970 and Projected for 1986 and 2000, Thailand

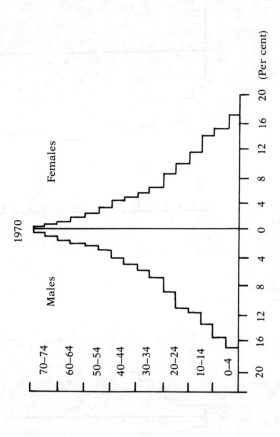

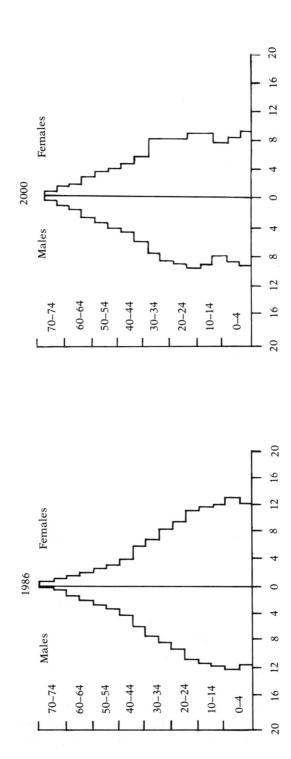

FIGURE 2.2 (Cont'd)

TABLE 2.2
Projected Proportion of Population Aged 65 and Over in 2025, ASEAN and Other Countries

	Population Aged 65 and Over (%)
Philippines	7.5
Indonesia	8.7
Thailand	9.1
Malaysia	9.1
China	12.9
Australia	15.9
Singapore	17.0
United States	17.2
United Kingdom	18.7
Canada	18.8
France	19.3
Italy	19.6
Sweden	22.2
Federal Republic of Germany	22.5
Switzerland	23.8
Japan	23.8

SOURCE: As for Table 2.1.

sent time. Furthermore, the rise in the share of the aged will have been very rapid indeed. Forty years from now, the proportion of elderly in the populations of Singapore, Indonesia, and Thailand will be three times as high as it is now. Table 2.3 shows that Singapore, like Japan, is expected to pass from 10 to 20 per cent elderly population (defining elderly as 65+) in less than a quarter century, and a very rapid transition can be expected in Thailand as well. By contrast, a transition taking more than half a century was more typical of the West.[3]

Particular problems can be expected to face the generation born immediately prior to the rapid decline in fertility. This generation is a very large one, constituting the base of the last high-fertility age pyramid in which succeeding birth cohorts were always larger than the one before, but left stranded, as it were, in the age structure by the undercutting of the pyramid below it by the sharp decline in fertility. In Singapore, this large cohort is the one born in the 1950s and early 1960s; in Thailand, it is the cohort born in the 1960s and early 1970s. This cohort

TABLE 2.3
International Comparison of the Speed of Population Ageing

	Year in which the Aged Population Reaches		Time Required to Increase from 10 to 20% (years)
	10%	20%	
Singapore	2012	2033	21
Japan	1985	2010	25
Finland	1973	2021	48
Netherlands	1968	2020	52
Federal Republic of Germany	1954	2010	56
Italy	1966	2027	61
Sweden	1945	2013	68
United Kingdom	1945	2031	86

SOURCES: As for Table 2.1 and U.N., *Demographic Yearbook*, various issues.

will produce relatively fewer children itself, and not only may it be unable to rely on assistance from children in old age because of their small number and the probable marginalization of the elderly within the family, but also as it enters the old ages it will cause a rapid jump in the proportion of the elderly in the total population, which will put a strain on the capacity (and even the willingness) of society as a whole to finance the growing needs of the elderly out of public (or, indeed, private) revenues. This financial "crunch" will occur in Singapore around the years 2020 to 2030 and in Thailand around the years 2030 to 2045.

Irrespective of what will happen to the *proportion* of elderly people in the population, the *absolute numbers* of old people will grow very rapidly in ASEAN countries over the remainder of this century. The fact that the proportion of old people will be rising in all ASEAN countries implies that the numbers of the old will grow more rapidly than the rest of the population. The trends are shown in Table 2.4. Since the decline in fertility will affect particularly the number of children it is the faster growth of the elderly than of the youthful population that is especially striking; however, except in the Philippines, the numbers in the working ages will also grow substantially less rapidly than the numbers of aged.

During the 20-year period, 1980–2000, the numbers of aged will approximately double in Indonesia and Thailand and in-

TABLE 2.4
**Relative Increase of the Aged (60 +) and Other Age Groups
in ASEAN Countries, 1980–2000**

	Percentage Increase				Absolute Increase of the Aged Population ('000)
	0–14	15–59	0–59	60 +	
Indonesia	6	60	36	105	8,379
Malaysia	15	69	47	83	655
Philippines	24	74	52	76	1,931
Singapore	−4	26	17	84	146
Thailand	4	63	38	92	2,314

SOURCE: As for Table 2.1.

crease by more than three-quarters in Singapore, the Philippines,
and Malaysia. Overall, in the ASEAN region, there will be 13.4
million more elderly people in the year 2000 than there were in
1980.

Even were rapid social and economic changes not taking
place in these countries, growth of this magnitude would require
careful planning to ensure that the situation of the aged was
being adequately catered for. In the context of rapid social and
economic changes, which could well mean that traditional support mechanisms can no longer be relied on, it is doubly important that forward planning be undertaken. The proportion of
the aged living in the cities will be increasing, and this means
that the proportion cut off from agriculture and home-grown
food supplies will also be increasing. In the cities, housing
arrangements can be less readily adjusted to cater to changing
family circumstances, and unavoidable costs (for transport,
utilities, food, etc.) can be higher than in rural areas, thus
making it difficult for the elderly poor to manage.

On the other side of the coin, in rapidly urbanizing countries,
it is often the young working-age population who migrate to
cities, leaving the elderly behind. The distorted age structure
which results in the rural areas brings particular problems for
the elderly, because of the breakdown of traditional family-
based communal activities. Such problems are a particular cause
for concern in Malaysia (Lim 1982; Strange 1980).

DEPENDENCY RATIOS

It would be unrealistic to look at the dependency burden represented by the aged in isolation. Both the elderly and children are dependants of those in the work-force. The main cause of an ageing population is declining fertility, and this is the reason why the increasing dependency burden of an ageing population is more than offset, for a considerable time at least, by a falling dependency burden of young people. This is shown in all the country projections in Figure 2.3. If young (<15) and old (60+) dependants are added together, the total dependency ratio (dependants/workers) falls steadily, because the slow increase in the old dependency ratio is more than offset by a rapid fall in the young dependency ratio. The drop in the overall ratio is very substantial: for example, in Indonesia from .80 in 1980 to .45 in the year 2020. Thereafter the dependency ratio rises once more, because the old dependency ratio begins to rise more steeply and the young dependency ratio barely changes. By about the year 2050, the overall dependency ratio will have climbed back almost to the level of .80, from which it began its decline in 1980.

The trends shown in this example are fairly standard for the early stages of the ageing process. Malaysia may still have 25 years, and Thailand and Indonesia 30 years, in which the dependency burden will become more favourable before the inevitable rise sets in. The Philippines may have as much as 40 years, as the total dependency ratio is expected to fall from .83 in 1980 to .47 in the year 2020.

Singapore, having undergone an earlier decline in fertility, is at a different point on the transition in dependency ratios than the other ASEAN countries. In 1980, the youth dependency ratio in Singapore had already fallen to .40, much lower than Indonesia's .74 or the Philippines' .77 at the same date. The sharp decline in the youth dependency ratio has already been achieved in Singapore, though the ratio is expected to decline further over the next decade, thereafter remaining essentially unchanged. Because of the slow but steady increase in the aged dependency ratio, the total dependency ratio will keep falling only until 1990 and thereafter begin to rise. This rise will ac-

DEPENDENCY RATIOS

It would be unrealistic to look at the dependency burden represented by the aged in isolation. Both the elderly and children are dependants on those in the work-force. The main cause of an ageing population is declining fertility, and this is the reason why the increasing dependency burden of an ageing population is more than offset, for a considerable time at least, by a falling dependency burden of young people. This is shown in all the country projections in Figure 2.3. If young (<15) and old (60+) dependants are added together, the total dependency ratio (dependants/workers) falls steadily, because the slow increase in the old-dependency ratio is more than offset by the rapid fall in the young-dependency ratio. The drop in the child ratio is very substantial; for example, in Indonesia from 75 in 1980 to 45 in the year 2020. Thereafter the dependency ratio rises once more, because the old dependency ratio begins to rise more steeply as the young dependency ratio barely changes. By about the year 2030, the overall dependency ratio will have climbed back almost to the level of 80, from which it began to decline in 1980.

The trends shown in this example are fairly standard for the early stages of the ageing process. Malaysia will still have 25 years, and Thailand and Indonesia 30 years, in which the dependency burden will become more favourable, before the inevitable rise sets in. The Philippines may have as much as 40 years, as the total dependency ratio is expected to fall from 83 in 1980 to 67 in the year 2020.

Singapore, having undergone an earlier decline in fertility, is at a different point in the transition in dependency ratios than the other ASEAN countries. In 1980, the youth dependency ratio in Singapore had already fallen to 40, much lower than Indonesia's 74 or the Philippines' 77 at the same date. The sharp decline in the youth dependency ratio has already been achieved in Singapore, though the ratio is expected to decline further over the next decade, thereafter remaining essentially unchanged. Because of the slow but steady increase in the aged dependency ratio, the total dependency ratio will keep falling only until 1990 and thereafter begin to rise. This rise will ac-

FIGURE 2.3
Dependency Ratios: Total, Young, and Old in
Indonesia, Malaysia, the Philippines, Singapore, and Thailand

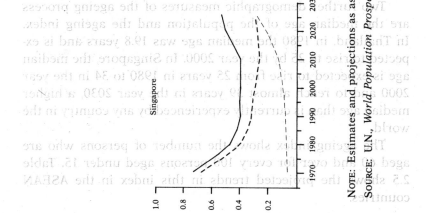

FIGURE 2.3 (Cont'd)

Dependency Ratios

Total = Population 0–14 + 65+ / Population 15–64

Young = Population 0–14 / Population 15–64

Old = Population 65+ / Population 15–64

Singapore

Thailand

NOTE: Estimates and projections as assessed in 1984.

SOURCE: U.N., *World Population Prospects* (New York: U.N., 1986).

celerate after the year 2010, due to an acceleration in the rise
of the aged dependency ratio.

Singapore is about 20 years ahead of Indonesia in its ageing process,[4] even assuming that fertility rates in Indonesia
will continue to decline rapidly. For example, the point at which
the aged dependency ratio will climb above the youth dependency ratio (that is, the point at which the number of old people
will first exceed the number of children) will occur 20 years
earlier in Singapore than in Indonesia (2025 compared with
2045). In the Philippines, this point is likely to be reached even
later than in Indonesia.

A decline in the total dependency ratio does not necessarily
mean that the dependency burden is lessening. It has been
estimated that in the United States, the per capita costs of the
elderly are about 3 times those of young people aged less than
15 years, and in Australia 2.3 times. So an elderly person puts
2 to 3 times as much demand on resources as a young dependant. This is unlikely to be the case in Indonesia because the
excess costs of the elderly in Western countries are largely
due to publicly-provided pensions. Even so, provided that the
elderly do cost somewhat more to support than the young, the
timing of the *real* about-turn in the dependency burden in Indonesia could be somewhat earlier than the year 2020 as shown
in Figure 2.3. On the other hand, it is not at all unlikely that the
retirement age in Indonesia will at some point be raised from
55 to 60, thereby modifying the impact of the dependency trends
shown in Figure 2.3.

Two further demographic measures of the ageing process
are the median age of the population and the ageing index.
In Thailand, in 1980 the median age was 19.8 years and is expected to rise to 25 by the year 2000. In Singapore, the median
age is expected to rise from 25 years in 1980 to 34 in the year
2000 and to reach almost 39 years in the year 2030, a higher
median age than is currently experienced by any country in the
world.

The ageing index shows the number of persons who are
aged 60 and over for every 100 persons aged under 15. Table
2.5 shows the projected trends in this index in the ASEAN
countries.

TABLE 2.5
Ageing Index* in ASEAN Countries, 1980–2020

	1980	1985	1990	1995	2000	2010	2020
Indonesia	12.9	14.6	17.5	20.8	24.9	33.2	48.4
Malaysia	14.5	15.1	16.4	18.5	23.1	34.9	53.3
Philippines	12.6	13.0	14.0	15.4	17.8	25.3	38.9
Singapore	26.6	32.0	37.6	42.5	51.2	78.2	117.8
Thailand	13.7	15.6	19.0	21.9	25.2	32.0	50.5

* $\dfrac{\text{Number of persons aged } 60+}{\text{Number of persons aged } 0\text{–}14} \times 100$

SOURCE: As for Table 2.1.

SEX RATIOS OF THE AGED

The preponderance of females at the extreme old ages has important implications for the kind of care needed by the aged, because elderly females are often widowed and lack financial resources that might have accrued from paid employment during their lifetimes.

Sex ratios at ages above 60, and the projected trends in sex ratios for the over 60 population in the ASEAN countries, are shown in Table 2.6. In Indonesia and Thailand, a relative deficiency of males is apparent at all ages above 60, and in Singapore at all ages above 70, whereas in Malaysia and the Philippines it is only at ages above 80 that a marked relative deficiency of males occurs. The sex ratio of the elderly in ASEAN countries as a whole is not as low as it is in Western countries,[5] presumably reflecting a history of high male war losses in Europe, Japan, and the Soviet Union and probably a lesser female advantage in survival chances throughout the adult ages in the ASEAN countries.

However, the projections, based on current age structure and mortality levels, do indicate that the relative excess of females in the old age groups will become more marked as time goes on (Table 2.7). By the year 2000, it appears that there will be fewer than 9 males for every 10 females at ages above 60 in all ASEAN countries, and in Malaysia, Singapore, and Thailand there will be fewer than 8 males for every 10 females.

TABLE 2.6
Sex Ratios* of the Aged in ASEAN Countries by Age, 1980

	60–64	65–69	70–74	75–79	80+
Indonesia	93	90	84	77	72
Malaysia	96	101	99	105	82
Philippines	70	95	96	101	82
Singapore	100	93	86	73	49
Thailand	90	90	76	72	57

*Sex Ratio $= \dfrac{\text{Males}}{\text{Females}} \times 100$

SOURCE: As for Table 2.1.

TABLE 2.7
**Projection of Sex Ratios* in the Population Aged 65+
in ASEAN Countries**

	1980	1990	2000	2010	2020
Indonesia	84	88	88	85	85
Malaysia	98	85	79	80	78
Philippines	95	87	85	86	85
Singapore	82	80	78	75	75
Thailand	78	79	78	78	80

*Sex Ratio $= \dfrac{\text{Males}}{\text{Females}} \times 100$

SOURCE: As for Table 2.1.

SHARE OF THE VERY OLD IN THE ELDERLY POPULATION

It is often found that the share of the very old (those aged 75+) in the old population (60+) rises as life expectancy is pushed upwards and people therefore tend to live longer after reaching old age. This trend is not, however, consistently evident in the projection for ASEAN countries (Table 2.8). In these countries a pronounced rise in the ratio of the old-old to the young-old, towards the higher levels of this ratio observed in Western countries (see Hauser 1983, Table 1), will have to wait on long-term changes in the age pyramid, because for many years to come the broad-based age pyramid generated by the earlier high-fertility regimes will be graduating successively larger cohorts into the younger segment of the aged population.

TABLE 2.8
Ratios of the Very Old to the Old (75 + /60 +) in ASEAN Countries

	1980	1985	1990	1995	2000	2010	2020
Indonesia	.151	.166	.172	.168	.172	.214	.216
Malaysia	.189	.219	.214	.222	.209	.206	.200
Philippines	.188	.183	.194	.194	.187	.186	.181
Singapore	.172	.203	.216	.215	.206	.206	.184
Thailand	.186	.199	.194	.187	.187	.206	.190

SOURCE: As for Table 2.1.

Notes

1. If the Philippine population continued to increase at its present rate, in less than 180 years it would be equal to that of the population of the entire world today, a quite ridiculous prospect.
2. Further mortality declines are assumed for Singapore, but for the "central projection", fertility is assumed to rise to replacement level by the year 2001 and thereafter remain constant.
3. It took a century in France for the proportion of the population aged 60 and over to rise from 8.9 to 12.7 per cent, then half a century to reach 16.2 per cent. In Singapore, the same two rises are expected to take 15 and 9 years, respectively. Admittedly, the ageing process in France took longer than in other European countries.
4. Interestingly enough, Singapore is in almost exactly the same situation in the ageing process as Japan. For evidence on Japan, see Kuroda and Hauser 1981.
5. The sex ratio at ages 65 + in 1980 was 63 in Japan, 79 in Northern America, and below 70 in Europe (Hauser 1983, Table 8).

3
CHARACTERISTICS OF THE AGED: A BRIEF OVERVIEW

Conditions vary very widely in the ASEAN region, and the circumstances of the region's elderly vary accordingly. This section will therefore provide a brief overview of these characteristics. Two main sources of information will be used: national censuses and surveys in which the elderly are enumerated along with the rest of the population; and special surveys of the elderly conducted in each country as part of the project on the Socio-Economic Consequences of the Ageing of the Population (hereafter referred to as ASEAN Ageing Surveys). The latter provide a unique set of data on many aspects of the family situation, living conditions, income, health, and recreation of the aged.

Differences between these two sources of data should be briefly noted. Firstly, the censuses refer to 1980 but the ASEAN Ageing Surveys to 1986 (except for the Philippines, where the survey was conducted in 1984). But more importantly, the censuses give either a complete count or a representative sample of all the elderly in the country, whereas among the ASEAN Ageing Surveys this is true only for Singapore and Thailand. In Malaysia, the survey is representative of the elderly in three west coast states of Peninsular Malaysia — Selangor, Negeri Sembilan, and Melaka. In Indonesia and the Philippines, the sample was chosen to give a broad cross-section of the elderly in various geographic areas and socio-economic groups, without any pretence at statistical representativeness. In Indonesia, the survey was confined to Java, which contains just over 60 per cent of the nation's population. Further details about sampling are given in the Appendix.

One limitation of the surveys is the omission of the elderly whose physical and mental conditions prevent them from being interviewed. This bias, however, is shared by virtually all research on the elderly (Treas and Logue 1986). Another limitation is the omission of the elderly who live in institutions, but this is not a serious omission as only a tiny proportion of the region's elderly live outside a household context.

Because of the differing degrees of representativeness of the census and survey data, the reader should take note of the source of each of the tables discussed in this section, listed at the foot of each table.

AGE AND SEX DISTRIBUTION

The percentage of the population aged 60 and over was already given in Table 2.1, and its sex ratios in Table 2.6. In the present section, the objective is to compare the age and sex composition of the elderly based on census data with the age and sex composition of the survey population in each of the ASEAN countries, to check whether the survey population diverges very much in this respect for the elderly population as a whole.

Table 3.1 shows that the age distribution within the group of elderly does not vary very much between countries. Over one-third of them are aged 60–64, a somewhat higher proportion are aged 65–74, and the "old-old" (aged 75+) constitute about one-fifth of all elderly. Females outnumber males among the elderly and most markedly among the "old-old". The female excess is less marked in Malaysia and Singapore, probably mainly because many of the elderly there are survivors of earlier, male-dominated immigration inflows.

Comparable data for the surveys (Table 3.2) do not show very marked differences from the census data in the age structure of the aged population. More marked differences do, however, show up in sex ratios. Sex ratios are higher in the survey than in the 1980 Census in Indonesia, but substantially lower in the surveys in Malaysia, the Philippines, and Thailand. There are many possible reasons for this greater representation of the female than of the male elderly in the surveys, including sampling variability, selective age or sex misstatement in either census or survey, and real changes due to the passage of time.

TABLE 3.1
Age and Sex Distribution of the Population Aged 60+, 1980

| | Percentage of Aged Population in Each Age Group | | | | | | | | | Sex Ratio* by Age | | | |
| | Males | | | Females | | | Both Sexes | | | | | | |
	60–64	65–74	75+	60–64	65–74	75+	60–64	65–74	75+	60–64	65–74	75+	All Ages 60+
Indonesia	41.6	40.0	18.4	39.3	41.0	19.7	40.4	40.6	19.0	93	86	82	87
Malaysia	36.0	45.5	18.5	36.4	44.3	19.3	36.2	44.9	18.9	97	100	93	97
Philippines	35.5	45.6	18.9	35.5	45.6	18.9	35.5	45.6	18.9	95	95	93	95
Singapore	36.7	48.4	14.9	32.3	46.9	20.8	34.4	47.6	18.0	100	90	63	87
Thailand	36.8	45.0	18.2	33.3	44.3	22.4	34.9	44.6	20.5	93	85	68	83

* Males per 100 females.

SOURCE: 1980 population censuses.

TABLE 3.2

Age and Sex Distribution of the Population Aged 60+, 1986

| | Percentage of Aged Population in Each Age Group | | | | | | | | | Sex Ratio by Age | | | |
| | Males | | | Females | | | Both Sexes | | | | | | |
	60–64	65–74	75+	60–64	65–74	75+	60–64	65–74	75+	60–64	65–74	75+	All Ages 60+
Indonesia	36.7	46.0	17.3	38.7	44.5	16.8	37.8	45.2	17.0	86	94	94	91
Malaysia	39.1	42.9	17.9	37.7	45.5	16.9	38.3	44.3	17.4	89	81	91	86
Philippines	38.3	43.4	18.2	32.5	45.8	21.7	35.1	44.7	20.1	96	77	68	81
Singapore	36.1	47.8	16.1	31.3	46.7	22.0	33.6	47.2	19.2	101	90	64	88
Thailand	32.5	46.9	20.6	33.8	43.8	22.4	33.2	45.1	21.7	67	74	64	69

SOURCE: ASEAN Ageing Surveys.

In any event, since most tables in this report present data separately for males and females, any discrepancy between the surveys and the census findings may cause a degree of bias only in the data combined for both sexes.

MARITAL STATUS

The proportion of the elderly who are currently married declines with age; the corollary of this is a rise in the proportion widowed (Table 3.3). But within any given age group, the proportion widowed among females is much higher than among males. (For example, in Indonesia, among those aged 75+, 77 per cent of males are married compared with 23 per cent of females). These sex differences are explained by three factors. First, males tend to marry females younger than themselves and are therefore less likely to have suffered the death of their spouse at any

TABLE 3.3
Marital Status of the Aged (60+) by Sex, 1980
(In percentages)

	Single	Married	Widowed	Divorced	Total
Indonesia					
Males	0.8	85.2	12.2	1.8	100
Females	1.0	31.0	62.4	5.6	100
Both sexes	0.9	56.4	38.9	3.8	100
Peninsular Malaysia					
Males	3.5	80.3	13.6	2.6	100
Females	2.1	37.1	53.9	6.9	100
Both sexes	2.7	57.7	34.6	5.0	100
Philippines					
Males	3.3	81.0	16.0	0.7	100
Females	7.9	50.4	40.6	1.0	100
Both sexes	5.5	65.3	28.4	0.8	100
Singapore					
Males	4.6	79.8	14.5	1.1	100
Females	5.0	37.2	56.8	1.0	100
Both sexes	4.8	57.1	37.0	1.1	100
Thailand					
Males	1.5	79.0	17.4	2.1	100
Females	2.1	41.8	53.1	2.9	100
Both sexes	1.9	58.7	36.9	2.5	100

SOURCE: 1980 population censuses.

given age than are females. Second, this differential is reinforced
by the tendency for mortality rates for males beyond middle age
to exceed those for females at the same ages. Third, widowed
males are more likely to remarry than are widowed females.

Some differences in marriage patterns between the countries are also reflected in the data: for example, the higher
incidence of divorce in Indonesia and of spinsterhood in the
Philippines. But the main point to note about marital status of
the elderly is the one already mentioned: the rise, with age, in
the proportion widowed, especially among females. Widowed
females constitute more than a quarter (29 per cent, to be exact)
of *all* old people in the ASEAN countries, and thus represent a
large enough group to justify special attention in planning programmes for the aged.

The marital status of the aged in the ASEAN Ageing Surveys
(Table 3.4) appears very close to that in the 1980 Census, with
the exception of females in the Philippines, of whom over 50 per
cent are currently married according to the census but only 33
per cent according to the survey.

The marital status of the elderly has an important bearing
on the family situation in which they live, to be discussed in the
following section.

FAMILY STRUCTURE OF THE AGED

From census reports for Indonesia and Thailand, it is possible
to discover something about the family contexts within which

TABLE 3.4
Marital Status of Respondents, 1986
(In percentages)

	Males		Females	
	Currently Married	Currently Not married	Currently Married	Currently Not married
Indonesia	87	13	33	67
Malaysia	85	15	31	69
Philippines	76	24	33	67
Singapore	84	16	33	67
Thailand	79	21	40	60

SOURCE: ASEAN Ageing Surveys.

the elderly live, through a table on relationship of respondents to the head of household. As shown in Table 3.5, a considerable proportion of the elderly in these countries are themselves the head of the household; although the male elderly are much more likely to be the head of household than are the female elderly. More relevant is the fact that the proportion of males who are the head of household greatly exceeds the proportion of females who are either head of household or the spouse of the head of household. This is directly related to the higher proportion of females who are widowed, most of whom appear to be living with their children's or children-in-laws' families. For example, in the Indonesian age group 65–74, 86 per cent of males were head of household compared with only 51 per cent of females who were either head or spouse of head of household. On the other hand, only 11 per cent of such males were the parent or parent-in-law of the head of household, compared with 40 per cent of such females. The female elderly were also more likely than the male elderly to be living with other relatives.

In these terms, then, the female elderly are much more commonly in a dependent status within the household than are the male elderly, but further light needs to be thrown on this status by comparing their sources of income or material support. This will be done in Chapter 5.

It is not easy to interpret the significance of the high rate of headship among the male elderly, as reported by censuses. The problem is the difference between *de facto* and *de jure* headship. As a person becomes very old, the real work, responsibility, and authority for running the household may devolve on, say, the married son living in the same household. But convention, and politeness, may decree that the old person is still regarded as official head of the household (Hetler 1986). Much probably depends on whether, in joint households, children are living in the house of the old person or whether the old person has moved into the house of children. In the latter case, there would not normally be a need, even in the *de jure* sense, to consider the old person as the head of the household. But as shown in Table 3.6, the majority of elderly respondents, except in Singapore, live in their own homes while others live in rented accommodation. Except in Singapore, only about 10 to 15 per cent are living in a house owned by other household members.

TABLE 3.5
Relationship to Head of Household by Age and Sex
(In percentages)

	Indonesia						Philippines	Thailand
	Head of Household	Parent/ Parent-in-Law	Other Relative	Servant	Others	Total	% Who Are Head of Household	% Who Are Head of Household
Males								
60–64	91.7	5.9	2.0	0.1	0.3	100	91	86
65–74	85.6	11.4	2.5	0.1	0.4	100	89	81
75+	70.9	24.1	4.0	0.1	0.9	100	70	66
All ages 60+	85.5	11.4	2.6	0.1	0.4	100	87	77
		(Wife)						
Females								
60–64	30.7	31.9	30.2	5.8	0.6	0.8	100	24	31
65–74	30.0	20.9	40.2	7.2	0.4	1.3	100	24	32
75+	25.0	8.9	52.8	10.4	0.3	2.6	100	25	30
All ages 60+	29.3	22.9	38.7	7.2	0.5	1.4	100	24	31

SOURCES: 1980 census reports and *1983 National Demographic Survey*, Philippines.

TABLE 3.6
Respondents' Ownership of House by Age and Sex, 1986
(In percentages)

	Indonesia			Malaysia			Philippines			Singapore	Thailand		
	U	R	T	U	R	T	U	R	T		U	R	T
Males													
60–64	79	91	87	57	77	71	54	97	74	62	71	96	92
65–74	77	91	86	47	78	71	60	98	82	45	57	91	86
75+	61	81	75	50	65	61	52	85	70	28	56	81	77
Total	76	89	84	52	75	69	56	95	77	48	61	91	86
Females													
60–64	27	41	36	59	71	68	57	86	70	36	61	94	87
65–74	38	43	41	57	65	62	49	84	66	22	48	83	77
75+	25	34	31	28	45	40	42	73	60	21	33	70	63
Total	31	41	37	53	64	61	51	82	66	31	49	83	77
Both Sexes													
60–64	51	64	60	58	74	69	56	92	72	49	65	95	89
65–74	59	65	63	53	71	66	53	91	73	38	52	86	81
75+	42	57	52	38	55	50	46	78	64	23	41	74	69
Total	53	63	60	52	70	65	53	88	71	39	54	86	81

NOTES: 1. U = Urban; R = Rural; T = Total.
2. "House owned by Respondent's Spouse" included in "House Owned by Respondent" in the case of all countries except Singapore.

SOURCE: ASEAN Ageing Surveys.

RESIDENCE, LITERACY, AND EDUCATION

Because most of their lives were lived before the period of dramatic economic and social development in the ASEAN region over the past two decades, the region's elderly came overwhelmingly from a rural background, even if they now live in cities in increasing numbers; and their levels of education are low. Except in Singapore, most still live in rural areas: 64 per cent in the Philippines, 82 per cent in Indonesia, 67 per cent in Malaysia, and 84 per cent in Thailand.

Literacy rates among the elderly are shown in Table 3.7. It is important, in designing programmes for the aged, to be aware that the great majority of elderly women are illiterate, and two-fifths to two-thirds of elderly men, depending on the country. Illiteracy among the elderly is more marked in rural than in urban areas. Literacy rates among the elderly will improve over time, as cohorts which grew up in times when educational facilities were improving reach old age. Nevertheless, even in the year 2000, a high proportion of elderly women (more than half of all elderly women in the dynamic city of Singapore, for example) will still be illiterate.

Related data are presented in Table 3.8 from the ASEAN Ageing Surveys. Three points emerge from this table. The first is that the proportion of the elderly population with secondary or post-secondary education is quite low. The second is that there is great international variability in this proportion, which ranges from 5.5 per cent in Thailand to 20.1 per cent in the Philippines. The third is that female educational levels are very much lower

TABLE 3.7
Literacy Rates among the Aged (60 +), 1980

	Males	Females	Both Sexes	Both Sexes Urban	Both Sexes Rural
Indonesia	44	14	28	44	25
Peninsular Malaysia*	43	9	26	36	21
Philippines	58	49	54	73	43
Singapore	69	20	43	43	0
Thailand	63	28	44	49	30

* A further 6 per cent of males and 3 per cent of females were "semi-literate".
SOURCE: ASEAN Ageing Surveys.

TABLE 3.8
**Respondents with Secondary or Post-Secondary Education
by Sex and Age Group**
(In percentages)

	Indonesia	Malaysia	Philippines	Singapore	Thailand*
Males					
60–64	9	30	37	33	11
65–74	8	19	21	23	12
75+	1	21	19	15	5
All ages 60+	7	24	27	25	11
Females					
60–64	3	6	19	8	4
65–74	2	4	15	5	1
75+	2	0	9	8	0
All ages 60+	2	4	15	7	2
Both Sexes					
60–64	6	18	28	20	7
65–74	5	11	17	14	6
75+	1	10	13	11	2
All ages 60+	5	13	20	16	5

* Grade 5+.
SOURCE: ASEAN Ageing Surveys.

than those of males. The Philippines has less of a sex differential than the other countries, but even here only 15 per cent of females have secondary education, compared with 26 per cent of males. But in a country such as Malaysia the difference is much more dramatic (4 per cent of females compared with 24 per cent of males).

LABOUR FORCE PARTICIPATION

It is normal for labour force participation rates to decline at older ages, though less rapidly in agricultural settings than in urban settings where wage employment is the norm. Labour force participation rates among the elderly in the ASEAN region are shown in Table 3.9. These rates, it will be noted, remain quite high at ages above the official retirement age, which serves to emphasize the point that only a small proportion of the population of the ASEAN countries (except Singapore) is in wage and salaried employment affected by compulsory retirement ages, and that in self-employment, economic necessity forces many people to continue working as long as they are able to, albeit

TABLE 3.9
**Labour Force Participation Rates
among Those Aged 60 +, 1980**

	60–64	65–69	70–74	75–79	80+	All Ages (60 +[a])	All Ages (60 +[b])
Males							
Indonesia	76.5	48.8	n.a.	---- 34.0 ----		48.5	63
Malaysia	69.4	------------ 49.7 ------------				56.8	57
Philippines[c]	89.9[d]	------------ 60.8 ------------				77.3[e]	56
Singapore[a]	47.3	32.1	21.4	15.4	9.3	32.1	28
Thailand	68.6	------------ 40.1 ------------				56.7	49
Females							
Indonesia	31.5	19.2	n.a.	------ 9.9 ----		21.6	36
Malaysia	26.7	------------ 19.0 ------------				21.8	27
Philippines[c]	45.0[d]	------------ 23.7 ------------				36.2[e]	25
Singapore[a]	10.3	8.9	6.5	3.0	1.4	7.7	9
Thailand	43.7	------------ 19.6 ------------				31.4	27

[a] Labour Force Survey, 1986.
[b] ASEAN Ageing Surveys.
[c] 1975.
[d] Refers to ages 55–64.
[e] Refers to ages 55 and above.
n.a. — Not available.

SOURCES: Philippines: Integrated Survey of Households, First Quarter 1983; other countries: 1980 population census.

sometimes at a reduced pace. In agriculture, where the bulk of the elderly workers are still to be found (Table 3.10), the pace of work can readily be adapted to the capabilities of the elderly, who in some cases may help out only in the busy seasons.

Labour force participation rates recorded from the ASEAN Ageing Surveys are recorded in the final column of Table 3.9. On the whole, they correspond quite closely with those shown by the censuses, although for Indonesia, the survey rates are substantially higher, for males and females. The types of occupation the working elderly have are shown in Table 3.10.

Table 3.11 shows the age of retirement for those who ever worked but are not currently working. There is a tendency for this to be more concentrated (in ages 55–64) in Singapore than in other countries, no doubt reflecting the higher proportion of Singapore workers in formal sector urban employment and therefore subject to official retirement ages. The table also shows a very wide range in the proportion of elderly females who were

TABLE 3.10
Occupation of Employed Persons Aged 60 +
(In percentages)

Occupation	Philippines*	Singapore	Thailand
Professional, technical, and related workers	2.7	2.6	0.7
Administrative, executive, and managerial workers	1.4	4.9	1.1
Clerical and related workers	1.2	5.8	0.5
Sales workers	8.8	29.3	12.9
Farmers, fishermen, hunters, loggers, etc.	70.9	6.3	75.1
Miners, quarrymen, etc.	0.2	n.a.	0
Transport and communication workers	1.2	n.a.	0.5
Craftsmen, production process workers	8.5	26.8	7.7
Service, sports, and related workers	3.6	24.2	1.5
Stevedores, freight handlers, etc.	1.1	n.a.	0
Not classifiable by occupation	0.5	0.1	0
Total	100	100	100

* 1975.
n.a. — Not available.
SOURCE: 1980 population censuses.

never in the work-force, from a low of 4 per cent in Thailand to a high of 51 per cent in Singapore.

Data from the Indonesian census of 1980 indicate that among those who are working, the hours of work gradually decrease as people grow older. For example, in urban areas, the proportion working fewer than 35 hours a week is 19 per cent for all workers, 30 per cent for those aged 60–64, and 42 per cent for those aged 65 and over. In rural areas, the comparable proportions are 41 per cent for all workers, 47 per cent for those aged 60–64, and 54 per cent for those aged 65 and over. Clearly, the effect of old age on hours of work is more marked in urban than in rural areas.

TABLE 3.11

Respondents by Activity Status and Retirement from Last Job

(In percentages)

	Males					Females				
	Indonesia	Malaysia	Philippines	Singapore	Thailand	Indonesia	Malaysia	Philippines	Singapore	Thailand
Presently working	63	43	56	28	49	36	17	25	9	27
Ever worked, retired at age:										
<45	1		2		1	2		18		4
45–54	6	} 57	9	} 9	5	6		11	} 15	12
55–64	15		19	52	25	18	} 61	19	20	31
65	12		14	11	20	13		11	5	22
Never worked	3	0	*	0	0	26	22	14	51	4
Total	100	100	100	100	100	100	100	100	100	100

* Less than 0.5 per cent.

NOTE: For Thailand, "Retirement age not known" was distributed between all ages.

SOURCE: ASEAN Ageing Surveys.

4
FAMILY RELATIONSHIPS AND AGEING

Every society must face the fundamental question of the appropriate extent of family responsibility for older people: for their emotional and financial support, living arrangements, and care when ill. This question needs to be examined in the context of sweeping changes in the economy and society that are everywhere leading to a redefinition of family life, and changes in family structure and functions. How does the increasing specialization and mobility of modern life affect the scope of family control? How do these family changes in turn affect the aged? "Ironically, modernization brings not only the greater longevity of old people but also changes in family size and composition that make family care more problematic" (Giele 1982, p. 43). Decreasing family size means fewer potential family caretakers for the elderly person, and the increasing tendency for married women to be in the paid work-force also works against their availability to care for the aged.

The impact of development on the position of the elderly has been the subject of considerable research and speculation (Treas and Logue 1986). A prominent view is that a general decline in the status of old people is associated with modernization (Cowgill and Holmes 1972), whereas others note the better income and care that well-paid workers can afford to give their parents or other aged relatives in modern society (Inkeles and Smith 1974). Cowgill (1974) singled out several factors associated with development — modern health technology, economic technology, urbanization, and increased education — and concluded that each tended to reduce the status of the elderly by depriving them of meaningful roles through early retirement, trapping them in more traditional and less rewarding jobs, separating them from their families, and lowering their social status relative to the young. At the same time, he recognized that several benefits accrued to the elderly from development, and observed that in the more economically developed countries, there was increasing attention to their needs and interests.

The relatively low proportion of old people who live with their children in Western societies should not necessarily be interpreted to mean that they are neglected. Older people in Western societies are increasingly able to be financially independent, due to their higher earning power in recent times and the widening coverage of pension and superannuation schemes. Many, indeed most, in these circumstances want to live independently, with what has been called "intimacy at a distance" (Giele 1982, p. 60).[1] Furthermore, as the share of the elderly in the total population rises, their political influence is likely to increase and hence their ability to extract benefits from government, particularly from elected governments (Preston 1984).

Processes of economic development in Southeast Asia certainly tend to marginalize the elderly in a number of respects. Family nucleation occurs, and husband, wife, and children no longer work together. The elderly may cease to have much of a role at all, either because they no longer live with their children, or because their experience appears outmoded in the context of technological and economic change and the higher levels of education of their children and grandchildren (see Kuroda and Hauser 1981, pp. 15–16). A grandfather whose offspring no longer depend on him for their income will soon cease to have any say in a wider range of matters affecting the family, including marriage decisions and occupational choice by the young.

Even so, a theory of economic determinism with respect to the role and status of the elderly would be misplaced. For example, cultural factors are clearly important in the family arrangements with respect to the elderly. In the mid-1970s, 28 per cent of elderly Australians (aged 65 and over) were living alone, compared with only 9 per cent of elderly Japanese (ESCAP 1981, p. 16). In Japan, almost four ageing persons out of five lived together with their children, as compared with less than one-quarter in the industrial nations in the West (Maeda 1978).

It is true that there were differences in the socio-economic situation in Japan and other Western countries, with respect to the housing situation, low levels of public old age support, and the lower proportion of older Japanese who never married or had children. Moreover, the proportion of people in Japan who expect to depend on their own children for eventual support is declining rapidly from more than half of the population in 1950 to under 20 per cent in 1969 (Petri 1982, p. 82). Nevertheless, cultural differences in family relationships no doubt also played a part in the much greater tendency for elderly Japanese to live with their children.

Within the ASEAN region, family relationships vary widely, not only because of different stages of economic development but also because of differences dating back to pre-industrial times. After all, all of the world's great religions and a number of the world's main ethnic groups are represented in the ASEAN countries, and the family structures deriving from these different backgrounds are naturally different. All of the ASEAN countries share a tradition of a close-knit family structure, but they differ in the extent to which individualism was traditionally allowed free rein, and there is no comprehensive information about the extent to which the aged lived with their children in earlier times.

Governments are increasingly intervening to provide programmes of housing, health care, social services, and income maintenance for the aged. A key question is the appropriate conditions for eligibility for various kinds of government support. Should only those persons without families be entitled to receive help? While providing aid to the elderly, how can governments encourage families to continue their own contributions and involvement?

There is evidence that the close-knit family may be a durable institution in ASEAN countries, just as in Japan, in the face of rapid demographic and economic change. If so, it should be possible for it to continue to play a major role in care for the aged. In Singapore, Wong and Kuo (1979) found that "the majority of our respondents maintain close contact with a tightly knit circle of relatives involving mostly parents and married offspring followed by siblings and in-laws". For all categories "there is a high affectual content". The small proportion of elderly who are residents of old people's homes had never married, or had married but been childless, or had no close kin. Those with kin are, on average, much older than the average age of residents as a whole. This suggests that for the aged with close family ties, admission to a home is sought only as a last resort, when frailty of mind and body imposes an intolerable burden of care.

The same appears to be true in the other ASEAN countries as well: homes for the aged are everywhere seen as a last resort for those who "fall between the cracks" because they are destitute and either have no relatives or are cut off from those they have, or because of disabilities that make them an intolerable burden on family care. (For a case study of those living in homes for the aged in Jakarta, see Adi 1982.) Surveys among the elderly cited in the individual country reports show a strong resistance to the idea of living in an old folks' home. For example, in Singapore, only 4 per cent of elderly respondents said they were willing to live in an old folks' home, 79 per cent were unwilling, and 16 per cent were undecided. In Indonesia, only 7 per cent were willing to live in an old folks' home and in Malaysia, 9 per cent. On the other hand, in the Philippines, a little more than 25 per cent of respondents said that homes for the aged are a "good idea" and that they would want to live in one if it were available in the province. The number of people in the ASEAN region actually living in old age homes is tiny (Table 4.1).

TABLE 4.1
**Number and Percentage of Old People Living
in Old People's Homes, 1980**

		Old People Living in Homes	
	Capacity	Number	%
Indonesia	5,000	n.a.	0.1
Peninsular Malaysia*	5,000	n.a.	0.4
Philippines	1,100	1,000	0.1
Singapore*	3,876	3,108	1.6
Thailand	1,350	1,327	0.1

n.a. — Not available.

* As at December 1984.

SOURCES: Social Research Center (1982) pp. 240–41; Singapore, Ministry of Health (1986); Department of Social Welfare and Development, Philippines.

AVAILABILITY OF KIN

The ASEAN Ageing Surveys enable us to determine how many living siblings and children the elderly respondents have. This is necessary background information for interpreting the data on living arrangements of respondents.

Table 4.2 shows the percentage distribution of respondents by number of siblings still living. These elderly respondents were born in times of high fertility, but relatively high mortality levels were also able to take their toll. Overall, however, three-quarters or more still had at least one living sibling in every country but Singapore, and one-quarter to one-half had three or more living siblings. The lower proportion in Singapore is a puzzle, because fertility levels in Singapore were high at the time these people were born, and subsequent mortality levels (with the important exception of World War II) lower than elsewhere in ASEAN. Possibly this reflects the higher proportion of migrants among the Singapore elderly. Some of them may still have siblings but living in other countries, and therefore feel that effectively they have no living siblings accessible to them.

Not surprisingly, the proportion with living siblings declines with advancing age, but even among respondents aged 75+, around two-thirds (except in Singapore) still had at least one living sibling.

Table 4.3 shows the percentage of respondents with different numbers of living children. Very few had no living children: 4 per cent or fewer in all countries but Indonesia, where the higher proportion of 8 per cent may reflect the relatively low fertility levels historically in Java, and the very high mortality rates in Indonesia until quite recent times. Table 4.3 may understate the proportion of respondents with three or more living children, but even so, three-quarters or more of respondents were still reported as having three or more living children, in all countries except Indonesia. The number declines somewhat with age, but remains at two-thirds or more in age group 75+.

The majority of respondents, then, do not lack for children to take care of them provided that their children are prepared to fulfil this role.

TABLE 4.2
Number of Siblings Still Alive
(In percentages)

	Indonesia			Malaysia			Philippines			Singapore			Thailand		
	0	1–2	3+	0	1–2	3+	0	1–2	3+	0	1–2	3+	0	1–2	3+
60–64	22	45	33	13	25	62	11	29	60	26	29	45	11	43	46
65–74	26	45	29	17	32	51	14	40	45	40	31	28	23	46	31
75+	39	44	17	34	40	26	32	41	27	56	34	10	36	50	14
All Ages	27	45	28	19	30	51	17	36	47	39	31	30	22	46	32

NOTE: In all countries except the Philippines, the category 1–2 could include three or more in cases where all siblings were of the same sex.

SOURCE: ASEAN Ageing Surveys.

TABLE 4.3
Respondents by Number of Children Still Alive
(In percentages)

	Indonesia			Malaysia			Philippines			Singapore			Thailand		
	None	1-2	3+*	None	1-2	3+*	None	1-2	3+*	None	1-2	3+*	None	1-2	3+*
60-64	8	33	59	1	14	85	3	13	84	3	21	76	3	19	78
65-74	7	36	57	2	15	83	4	17	79	4	17	79	4	21	75
75+	9	40	51	3	15	82	7	22	71	7	30	63	4	27	69
All Ages	8	35	57	2	15	83	4	17	79	4	21	75	4	22	74

* 3+ is supposed to be "including at least one of each sex", so 1-2 could include more than two if all children were of the same sex.

SOURCE: ASEAN Ageing Surveys.

LIVING ARRANGEMENTS OF THE ELDERLY

Both the W.H.O. Survey on Health Care of the Elderly (Andrews et al. 1985) and the ASEAN Ageing Surveys give information on the living arrangements of respondents. They show that in Malaysia, the Philippines, and Singapore, very few of the elderly live alone (6 per cent in Malaysia, 3 per cent in the Philippines, and 2 per cent in Singapore; the figure reaches 8 per cent in Indonesia). Fewer than 10 per cent of respondents in Malaysia, the Philippines, and Indonesia are living alone or with non-relatives.

An important element of living arrangements is whether the old person is living together with his or her spouse, whether or not in the company of others. The presence of the spouse in the household has an important bearing on well-being, and in this sense elderly males are much better placed than elderly females: approximately three-quarters of elderly males have their spouse present in the household, compared with only about 30 per cent of elderly females (Table 4.4).

The great majority of the elderly (over 70 per cent of both males and females in all four countries) are living with one or more of their children (Table 4.4). Moreover, the family provides their means of financial support in a substantial proportion of cases, especially in the case of females, because few females have employment or pension incomes to fall back on. Their close integration into a family group is presumably the reason why in the W.H.O. survey, few elderly respondents (about 10 per cent in Malaysia and 5 per cent in the Philippines) "felt lonely" and why even fewer (1 per cent in Malaysia, 0 per cent in the Philippines) said they had no help if ill. However, the ASEAN Ageing Surveys show a different pattern: in the Philippines, 51 per cent, and in Thailand 18 per cent, of the elderly respondents cited loneliness as one of their most serious problems.

ROLE OF CHILDREN IN OLD AGE SECURITY

Children provide a major source of old age security in most Asian countries, and this has been seen as a major barrier to fertility decline in the absence of very effective social security systems (see, for example, Nugent 1985, for a general review of

TABLE 4.4
Living Arrangements of Respondents

	Indonesia	Malaysia	Philippines	Singapore
Males				
Live alone	1.9	3.8	2.0	1.7
Live with spouse only	20.0	14.1	6.3	⎫ 80.6
Live with spouse and other family members	60.3	65.7*	67.1	⎭
Live with other family members	17.2	14.1	24.5	8.9
Live with others (non-family)	0.7	2.3	0.2	8.8
Total	100	100	100	100
Females				
Live alone	13.5	8.7	3.7	2.8
Live with spouse only	10.5	5.8	3.6	⎫ 31.0
Live with spouse and other family members	16.9	22.5*	28.0	⎭
Live with other family members	56.8	61.3	64.5	54.3
Live with others (non-family)	2.2	1.7	0.3	11.9
Total	100	100	100	100
Both Sexes				
Live alone	8.0	6.4	3.0	2.3
Live with spouse only	15.0	9.7	4.8	⎫ 54.2
Live with spouse and other family members	37.6	42.4	45.5	⎭
Live with other family members	37.9	39.5	46.6	33.0
Live with others (non-family)	1.5	2.0	0.2	10.5
Total	100	100	100	100

* Includes a small number (less than 1 per cent) of those who live with spouse plus others (non-family).

SOURCE: ASEAN Ageing Surveys.

the literature, and Cain 1986, on South Asia). Nevertheless, in most ASEAN countries, fertility *has* fallen markedly, indicating that other considerations must have overwhelmed the old-age security motive for having large families. In any case, one would expect the old-age security motive to differ in intensity between different societies even when their economic situation is similar.

In this context, indicators of children's economic roles in various countries, most of them Asian countries in the earlier stages of the fertility transition and other Asian and Western countries much further through the transition, are of considerable interest (Table 4.5). Some of the key points to emerge from this table are as follows:

1. Expectations of help in old age declined in salience across countries as fertility fell. They only declined slightly between high-fertility and moderate-fertility countries, but declined much more sharply between moderate-fertility and low-fertility countries.

2. Expectations of wives and husbands showed parallel declines.

3. "To depend on when old" as a reason for having children received strongly negative ratings in low-fertility countries.

4. The percentage expecting support in old age from sons fell off substantially only in low-fertility countries (Singapore and the United States). The percentage expecting help from daughters was also relatively low in Korea and Taiwan.

5. Comparison between the higher- and lower-fertility regions of the Philippines and Korea (not shown) by and large show similar patterns. In the Philippines the patterns are not very clear-cut, but then the fertility differences between the regions compared are not very great. Perhaps more interesting is the finding (not shown in Table 4.5) that in Korea, Japan, the Philippines, and Thailand only 40 per cent of the urban middle-class respondents expected to be cared for by family members in old age, compared with 68 per cent of the urban lower classes and 83 per cent of the rural respondents.

Thus Table 4.5 shows, on the whole, the expected decline in the old-age security motive for having children in countries as fertility is lowered, and lowered expectations of help from children, either as they are growing up or later, when the parents grow old. Since the fertility declines are correlated with economic development, we might tentatively conclude that ASEAN countries will probably follow Western patterns whereby, with economic development, many parents neither expect nor receive economic or other forms of assistance from their children in old age.

Many commentators on the status of the aged in the ASEAN region show concern about the changing situation of the elderly in the context of rapid socio-economic change in the region. Singh (1983) notes that in Peninsular Malaysia, "it has always been considered a source of pride to have elderly parents and grand-parents residing in one's home". But he argues that rapid socio-economic change is affecting attitudes towards the elderly. Rural-urban migration is leading to a rise in the share of the elderly to the total population in many rural areas; the rapid rise in educational levels among the younger generation creates a sense of insecurity amongst the elderly, who feel a loss of status at being unable to cope with the rapid advance in knowledge attained by the young; higher work-force participation by young women is eroding one source of home care for the elderly; and there is an increasing tendency for young people to move into their own house soon after marriage, isolating the aged from younger family members in more than just the physical sense. Chan (1983) argues that sex differentials in old age mortality pose great problems for elderly widows because Malaysian society still retains its traditional emotional and psychological dependence of females on males. The importance of all these factors can be expected to intensify as the population of Malaysia continues to age in coming years.

The Report of the Secretary General to the World Assembly on Ageing in 1982 made the following recommendation:

> In view of the family's importance to the ageing, social policies should concentrate on those who provide assistance for the ageing, and since this role is often played by the family, some form of relief should be provided so that families are not indirectly penalised by society for caring for the aged. A clear and premeditated social policy, through income maintenance schemes or similar arrangements, should be established to provide support for those families who give assistance to their ageing members on a long-term basis. . . . Assistance in particular should be given to families that could be over-burdened by a

TABLE 4.5

Indicators of Children's Economic Roles by Country and Sex of Respondents, 1975–76

Indicator	Country (Crude Birth Rate, 1976)								
	Philippines (41)	Turkey (39)	Indonesia (38)	Thailand (29)	Korea (23)	Taiwan (20)	Singapore (13)	United States (10)	West Germany (10)
WIVES									
Percentage Mentioning Advantages									
Help in housework	35	11	33	9	3	4	9	3	0
Help in old age	44	43	60	27	23	30	41	7	10
Financial, practical help	49	22	53	54	26	17	13	2	1
Ratings[a] of Reasons for Having Children									
To work and help	.11	.06	.06	.04	-.31	-.25	-.18	-.50	-.37
To depend on when old	.20	.24	.13	.31	.06	.14	.30	-.48	-.41
Percentage Expecting Help from Sons									
Help around house	83	65	81	73	82	68	39	85	n.a.
Support in old age	86	93	82	89	85	85	39	12	n.a.
Part of salary	67	77	60	71	71	76	38	29	n.a.
Contribution in emergencies	88	95	83	92	87	92	58	74	n.a.
Support for siblings' schooling	84	87	81	86	65	83	44	13	n.a.
Percentage Expecting Help from Daughters									
Help around house	94	94	92	96	84	82	55	92	n.a.
Support in old age	85	81	77	87	46	39	31	11	n.a.
Part of salary	68	60	56	58	59	72	32	29	n.a.
Contribution in emergencies	88	85	81	89	75	88	49	73	n.a.
Support for siblings' schooling	84	76	72	83	59	79	39	13	n.a.
(Number of respondents)[b]	(1,691)	(1,760)	(2,034)	(2,614)	(1,565)	(2,217)	(977)	(1,569)	(296)

TABLE 4.5 (*Cont'd*)

Indicator	Country (Crude Birth Rate, 1976)								
	Philippines (41)	Turkey (39)	Indonesia (38)	Thailand (29)	Korea (23)	Taiwan (20)	Singapore (13)	United States (10)	West Germany (10)
HUSBANDS									
Percentage Mentioning Advantages									
Help in housework	31	8	16	7	2	3	4	2	n.a.
Help in old age	29	44	48	28	20	30	36	8	n.a.
Financial, practical help	53	23	56	51	22	22	11	4	n.a.
Ratings[a] of Reasons for Having Children									
To work and help	.10	−.04	.05	.06	−.27	−.30	−.31	−.46	n.a.
To depend on when old	.17	.24	.11	.28	.06	.07	.25	−.51	n.a.
Percentage Expecting Help from Sons									
Help around house	86	80	89	73	82	67	33	87	n.a.
Support in old age	82	88	82	78	79	76	31	12	n.a.
Part of salary	61	67	52	53	63	52	29	19	n.a.
Contribution in emergencies	85	88	81	87	81	86	49	66	n.a.
Support for siblings' schooling	83	87	81	82	60	79	35	16	n.a.
Percentage Expecting Help from Daughters									
Help around house	92	91	93	92	80	79	48	90	n.a.
Support in old age	80	67	81	75	43	29	26	11	n.a.
Part of salary	61	27	50	49	42	57	24	18	n.a.
Contribution in emergencies	84	62	80	84	66	80	43	65	n.a.
Support for siblings' schooling	80	67	80	77	52	74	31	15	n.a.
(Number of respondents)[b]	(382)	(545)	(983)	(1,311)	(490)	(1,023)	(491)	(456)	(0)

n.a. — Not applicable to West German sample.

[a] Deviations from the mean rating assigned by each individual to all 19 reasons. Original ratings were on a scale from 1 (not important) to 3 (very important).

[b] Because of missing data, some percentages and means are based on slightly fewer respondents.

Source: Derived from Bulatao (1979, Table 4).

disabled or chronically sick ageing member, and counselling services
for these situations should be provided. (U.N. 1982, p. 11)

Although there is no need to assume that the experience of
the West will necessarily be followed in ASEAN countries as
they age, it is important to realize that traditional family relationships will be put under great pressure by the demographic
changes expected to take place. Forty years from now, the proportion of elderly in the population of Singapore, Indonesia,
and Thailand will be three times as high as it is now, and micro-
demographic changes will mirror these trends, implying a steep
rise in the number of aged dependants per potential caregiver.
In Indonesia, if the nation's goals for fertility and mortality
decline are met, the current situation in which middle-aged
parents can expect to have about four living children available
to support them in their old age will be replaced within forty
years by a situation in which elderly people are likely to have
only two or three living children, who in turn may have living
grandparents as well to support. A small, though growing, proportion may have no children, either because they remained un-
married or remained childless. Of course, these changes will
not occur instantaneously, and adjustments will be taking place
throughout the intervening period.

Notes

1. As a recent American study notes,

> the price paid for strong family ties by family members in develop-
> ing countries around the world is a substantial loss of autonomy.
> It is a price most American grandparents are not willing to pay.
> (Cherlin and Furstenberg 1986)

5
EMPLOYMENT AND FINANCIAL SUPPORT OF THE AGED

It was noted earlier that most of the aged who work in ASEAN countries except Singapore are in agriculture, and that the decline in labour force participation rates as age increases is only very gradual. As shown in Tables 5.1 to 5.3, the rates are universally higher in rural than in urban areas. This probably reflects, not so much the need for the aged to work, but rather the integrated household economy in the rural areas, in which the elderly play a variety of roles. These include continued participation in the management of and actual physical work in the farm holding, in return for their support from the proceeds of the household's economic activities, support which normally continues after they have become too old to perform any economically productive activities.

Table 5.4, showing the reasons for stopping work among those who have stopped, supports this general thesis. Aside from the reason "reached retirement age", which was particularly important for males in Singapore and the Philippines and probably reflects mainly formal sector government and private employment, the main reason given for stopping work was "ill health". This would certainly not be the case in Western societies, where standard retirement ages apply and pension systems then take effect, and where the proportion of the workforce who are employees is much higher. But in ASEAN countries, some level of involvement in the work-force is normal until increased ill health related to ageing makes this no longer

TABLE 5.1
Respondents Not Working by Age and Sex
(In percentages)

	Indonesia	Malaysia	Philippines	Singapore	Thailand	
					Last Week	Last Year
Males						
60–64	26	47	35	60	45	30
65–74	37	59	41	76	62	53
75+	62	78	71	85	78	73
All ages	37	58	44	72	60	49
Females						
60–64	53	74	65	86	66	53
65–74	67	87	75	92	77	74
75+	84	92	87	97	92	91
All ages	64	83	75	91	77	70
Both Sexes						
60–64	40	62	50	73	57	44
65–74	52	75	61	84	71	65
75+	73	82	81	92	87	84
All ages	51	72	61	82	70	62

SOURCE: ASEAN Ageing Surveys.

TABLE 5.2
Urban Respondents Not Working by Age and Sex
(In percentages)

	Indonesia	Malaysia	Philippines	Singapore	Thailand	
					Last Week	Last Year
Males						
60–64	39	65	57	60	60	60
65–74	47	77	64	76	71	68
75+	63	77	81	85	84	83
All ages	47	72	64	72	70	68
Females						
60–64	63	90	68	86	80	72
65–74	76	94	82	92	80	80
75+	88	100	89	97	94	91
All ages	73	94	78	91	83	80
Both Sexes						
60–64	52	79	63	73	73	68
65–74	61	88	75	84	77	75
75+	76	89	86	92	90	88
All ages	60	84	72	82	78	75

SOURCE: ASEAN Ageing Surveys.

TABLE 5.3
Rural Respondents Not Working by Age and Sex
(In percentages)

	Indonesia	Malaysia	Philippines	Thailand	
				Last Week	Last Year
Males					
60–64	19	41	10	42	24
65–74	30	54	24	60	50
75+	63	78	63	77	72
All ages	32	53	27	58	46
Females					
60–64	47	68	60	62	49
65–74	63	84	68	76	72
75+	81	89	86	92	91
All ages	60	79	70	75	68
Both Sexes					
60–64	34	55	35	54	39
65–74	48	70	47	69	63
75+	72	83	77	86	83
All ages	47	66	50	68	59

* In Singapore there were no areas considered to be rural.
SOURCE: ASEAN Ageing Surveys.

possible. This continued involvement in the work-force helps provide the justification for the aged to maintain their status as head of household.

Table 5.5 (for Thailand and the Philippines) confirms the tendency for old people in these societies to continue to work as long as they are physically capable of it. Even among the group aged 75+, around half of all respondents wanted to work.

SOURCES OF FINANCIAL SUPPORT

In Western countries, social security is the most prevalent source of income for aged individuals. For example, in the United States, in 1974 over 90 per cent of all families whose head was 65 years old or older were receiving social security benefits. Approximately 70 per cent were receiving income either from private pensions, annuities, or other forms of privately attained "unearned" income. Income from accumulated assets, from drawing down their stock of wealth, or from current earnings

TABLE 5.4

Respondents' Reasons for Stopping Work by Sex

(In percentages)

Reason	Indonesia		Philippines		Singapore		Thailand	
	Males	Females	Males	Females	Males	Females	Males	Females
Reached retirement age	28	4	42	4	45	14	10	1
Enough financial means	*	*	n.a.	n.a.	1	8	} 8	} 13
Children do not allow	2	15	4	8	5	12		
Ill health	46	45	46	63	23	13	74	75
Domestic reasons	4	8	1	6	5	20	} 8	} 11
Have worked enough	3	4	n.a.	n.a.	6	10		
Other	18	24	7	19	18	23		
Total	100	100	100	100	100	100	100	100

* Less than 0.5 per cent.

n.a. — Not available.

NOTE: No data were available for Malaysia.

SOURCE: ASEAN Ageing Surveys.

TABLE 5.5
**Total Aged Respondents Who Want to Work
(Including Those Working), Thailand and the Philippines**
(In percentages)

	Thailand		Philippines	
	Males	Females	Males	Females
60–64	80.1	70.8	62.5	53.4
65–74	71.8	61.0	59.0	49.4
75+	58.3	48.2	46.0	44.4
All Ages	71.7	61.5	56.3	49.5

SOURCE: Napaporn Chayovan and Malinee Wongsith (1987).

were also part of many elderly people's income sources (Clark and Spengler 1980, p. 54). Direct income support from family members is so unimportant that it is not even mentioned in a recent book on the economics of population ageing in the United States (Clark and Spengler 1980).

The situation in ASEAN countries is very different. Respondents in the ASEAN Ageing Surveys were asked whether they received certain kinds of monetary or material support, and what was their main source of such support. The pattern differed somewhat by country, and differed considerably by sex. As can be seen in Table 5.6, children or grandchildren were the main source of material support for the large majority of elderly women, though in Indonesia and Thailand income from their own economic activity was the main source of support in a substantial number of cases. For men, the role of children and grandchildren was less, but in Singapore and Malaysia they were nevertheless the main source of support. Income from their own economic activity and from pensions and provident funds was also more important for men than for women.

Table 5.7 shows the proportion of respondents who were receiving various kinds of material support, not necessarily as the main source of support. Again, the role of children and grandchildren is emphasized by the high proportions mentioning this source of support, although a substantial proportion of male respondents also mentioned income from economic activity or from pensions and provident funds.

Additional tables for urban and rural areas (Tables 5.8 and

TABLE 5.6
Respondents' Main Source of Material Support by Sex
(In percentages)

Main Source of Support	Indonesia		Malaysia		Singapore		Thailand	
	Males	Females	Males	Females	Males	Females	Males	Females
Salaries, business	56	30	36	12	25	7	40	21
Interest, dividends, rent	2	1	3	2	1	1	0	0
Pension/Provident fund	13	4	16	6	9	1	5	1
Husband/Wife	4	11	2	7	2	6	1	2
Children/Grandchildren	22	47	38	67	53	80	38	54
Other relatives	1	5	1	2	0	1	2	4
Friends	0	*	0	*	0	0	0	0
Government agencies	*	0	2	2	0	0	0	0
Charity organizations (private)	0	0	*	*	0	0	0	0
Own savings	0	0	0	0	9	3	8	8
Others	1	1	2	1	1	1	6	10
Total	100	100	100	100	100	100	100	100

* Less than 0.5 per cent.
SOURCE: ASEAN Ageing Surveys.

TABLE 5.7
Respondents Receiving Certain Kinds of Monetary/Material Support
(In percentages)

Source of Support	Indonesia		Malaysia		Philippines		Singapore	
	Males	Females	Males	Females	Males	Females	Males	Females
Salaries, business	61	34	49	21	79[a]	49[a]	30	9
Interest, dividends, rent	5	3	16	7	1	3	12	5
Pension/Provident fund	16	5	21	8	18	9	29	6
Husband/Wife	11	14	7	15	6	11	5	11
Children/Grandchildren	56	70	76	90	39	52	80	91
Other relatives	5	12	7	10	3	8	4	4
Friends	1	1	2	3	1	[b]	2	2
Government agencies	[b]	[b]	6	4	0	[b]	0	0
Charity organizations (private)	[b]	[b]	6	9	0	0	0	0
Others (own savings)	3	3	5	2	0	2	46	29

[a] Regrouping of categories may have resulted in some double counting.
[b] Less than 0.5 per cent.

NOTE: Respondents could cite more than one source.

SOURCE: ASEAN Ageing Surveys.

5.9) show that in urban areas, pensions or provident funds provide the main source of material support in a higher percentage
of cases, reaching over 20 per cent for males in Malaysia, Thailand, and Indonesia. In rural areas, the importance of "salaries,
business" as the main source of support increases, but there is
some difficulty in interpreting these figures. In some cases the
old person's contribution to the enterprise (often the family farm)
may be relatively small and to categorize their income thus may
disguise a considerable financial contribution from family
members. The force of this comment is increased when we note
that in Table 5.6, it is in Singapore, the most urbanized country
in the region, that the reliance on children/grandchildren as the
main source of material support is the greatest. In the other countries, the real contribution of children in supporting parents is
almost certainly underestimated as a result of old people's status
as head of household, thus entitling them to feel that they had
a part in the farm or business from which they were supported,
even if they were no longer doing much, if any, real work. In
Thailand, when asked whether they needed financial and other
assistance from children, 86 per cent of elderly males and 91
per cent of elderly females replied in the affirmative (Chayovan
and Wongsith 1987, Table 12).

In any case, it is clear that even in countries where provident
funds currently cover most of the work-force (Singapore and
Malaysia), a much lower proportion of the elderly were in such
schemes during their working years. In the Philippines, where
53 per cent of workers are currently covered by the social
security system, only 8 per cent of the aged population is receiving pensions from this system. Therefore it falls on the family
to play a key role in the financial support of the aged, with
government intervening as little as possible to provide support
for the small group which is truly destitute.

Data from the National Survey on Senior Citizens, conducted
in Singapore in 1982, demonstrates more clearly than Tables 5.6
to 5.9 the nearly universal financial support provided to the
elderly by family members. Some data from this survey are
presented in Table 5.10. What is striking is not so much the high
proportion of those without their own source of income who
receive assistance from family members, but the high proportion of those with their own source of income (two-thirds of

TABLE 5.8

Main Source of Material Support by Sex, Urban Areas

(In percentages)

Main Source of Support	Indonesia		Malaysia		Singapore		Thailand	
	Males	Females	Males	Females	Males	Females	Males	Females
Salaries, business	46	23	24	6	25	7	24	13
Interest, dividends, rent	2	2	5	3	1	1	0	0
Pension/Provident fund	26	10	23	8	9	1	19	3
Husband/Wife	4	15	1	12	2	6	2	3
Children/Grandchildren	19	43	41	66	53	80	40	59
Other relatives	1	5	2	3	0	1	3	4
Friends	0	a	0	1	0	0	0	0
Government agencies	0	0	0	0	0	0	0	0
Charity organizations (private)	0	0	b	b	0	0	0	0
Own savings	0	0	b		9	3	9	10
Others	1	1	4	1	1	1	3	8
Total	100	100	100	100	100	100	100	100

[a] Less than 0.5 per cent.

[b] Included in "others".

NOTE: No data are available for the Philippines.

SOURCE: ASEAN Ageing Surveys.

TABLE 5.9

Main Source of Material Support by Sex, Rural Areas

(In percentages)

Main Source of Support	Indonesia		Malaysia		Thailand	
	Males	Females	Males	Females	Males	Females
Salaries, business	62	33	41	14	43	22
Interest, dividends, rent	2	1	2	2	0	0
Pension/Provident fund	6		14	5	2	0
Husband/Wife	4	8	2	5	1	2
Children/Grandchildren	24	49	37	67	37	54
Other relatives	1	5	1	2	2	4
Friends	0	*	0	*	0	0
Government agencies	0	0	2	3	0	0
Charity organizations (private)	*	0	*	1	0	0
Own savings	0	0	0	0	8	8
Others	2	2	1	1	7	10
Total	100	100	100	100	100	100

* Less than 0.5 per cent.

NOTE: No data are available for the Philippines.

SOURCE: ASEAN Ageing Surveys.

TABLE 5.10

Elderly Persons by Age Group, Sex, and Own Monetary Income, Singapore

(In percentages)

Sex/Age Group	Source of Own Income					
	Salaries/Business Income Only	Interest, Dividends, Rent Only	Pension Only	More than 1 Source	Nil	Total
Males						
60–69	42.4	11.3	2.5	13.0	30.8	100.0
70–79	24.8	10.9	3.5	9.1	51.7	100.0
80 and above	13.6	11.0	2.5	3.4	69.5	100.0
All males	35.1	11.2	2.8	11.2	39.7	100.0
Females						
60–69	11.9	11.9	0.7	3.8	71.8	100.0
70–79	5.5	11.4	0.4	1.2	81.5	100.0
80 and above	1.4	5.7	1.9	0.5	90.5	100.0
All females	8.8	11.1	0.7	2.6	76.8	100.0

SOURCE: Singapore, Ministry of Social Affairs (1983).

males; four-fifths of females) who still receive cash contributions
from relatives. An almost equal proportion receive, in addition,
maintenance in kind. It is likely, of course, that in many cases
those "with own source of income" do not have enough income
to support themselves fully.

Is the almost universal provision of financial and other support to the aged by their children in ASEAN countries the result
of an inherently close family structure built on respect for the
elderly and a high degree of altruism, or are there certain
enforcement mechanisms also at work?

This raises complex questions about the extent of economic
determinism of family systems. But it is clear that the aged do
maintain some levers of control which help to ensure that support will be forthcoming. Ownership of the house, reported on
in Chapter 3, appears to be one. In rural Java, it is common for
old people to delay bequeathing the house, housegarden, and
land to their children until they die (Sunarto 1978), thus effectively retaining control of the household economy. If they do
transfer the land before this, it is often accompanied by a specific
agreement by the children to make provision for the parents'
needs, and where such an agreement is not made, quarrels and
unhappiness often result (White 1976, Chapter 9).

Interestingly, a very similar situation is portrayed in a study
in Bangladesh (Chaudhury 1982, pp. 95–96), which found that
the great majority of elderly parents had not distributed their
land among their children. Control over land is a powerful
mechanism through which parents control the labour of their
children and ensure economic support in old age and participation in family decision-making.

The issue of control of house and land will undoubtedly
lead to further tensions as Indonesian society changes, because
parents who lose control of the family's source of livelihood do
not enjoy the position of dependency in which it places them,
but neither do children whose parents retain control enjoy the
status of "eternal apprentice" in their adult years.

FORMAL SOCIAL SECURITY SYSTEMS: THEIR LINKS TO CAPACITY OF THE ECONOMY TO PAY

ASEAN economies range all the way from the industrial (Singapore) to the agricultural (Indonesia and Thailand), with a wide range of historical and cultural backgrounds as well. These diverse backgrounds could be expected to influence the extent to which they have managed to provide systems of social security that give old people a degree of financial independence and choice of living arrangements. Table 5.11 summarizes data on this.

Two main points should be emphasized. First, there is a remarkably wide range in the coverage of pensions, superannuation, or Central Provident Fund schemes, from around 80 per cent of the labour force in Singapore and Malaysia to only about 3 per cent in Thailand. International experience shows that it is not until countries reach reasonably high levels of per capita income that a substantial share of the GNP goes into pension schemes. ASEAN experience is consistent with this: it is only Singapore and Malaysia that a substantial share of GNP is devoted to such schemes: 1.22 per cent and 0.58 per cent, respectively, both still well below the figure 5.5 per cent in industrialized countries (Petri 1982, Appendix 1).

Secondly, most old-age security schemes in the region are compulsory income contributory schemes rather than taxation-based pension schemes. Though this avoids some of the problems of pay-as-you-go schemes, it also misses some of their benefits, such as an assured income for the elderly poor who were never employees (a group which is very large).

Central Provident Fund (CPF) schemes operate in both Singapore and Malaysia. For all employees, a compulsory contribution is deducted every month from the employee and employer and deposited into a personal account with the Central Provident Fund Board (or, in Malaysia, the Employees Provident Fund [EPF]). Some of the savings can be put towards the purchase of a house or, in Singapore, purchase of approved shares. A member can withdraw part or all of the accumulated credit on attaining the age of 55 (50 or 55 in Malaysia).

In Singapore, CPF members have two accounts — an Ordinary Account and a Special Account. Both accounts earn interest, but whereas savings in the Special Account are withdrawable only on attainment of age 55 or for special contingencies, savings in the Ordinary Account can be withdrawn under the various CPF schemes for the purchase of residential proper-

TABLE 5.11
Pensions and Old Age Insurance

Country	Beneficiaries	Number of Employees Covered	Working Population Covered (%)	Notes
Indonesia	Civil servants including armed forces and industrial workers.	6 million	11.5	Lump sum provident fund paid on retirement.
Thailand	Civil servants and some private sector employees.	54,535 (1985)	About 3	Social insurance bill proposed in 1982, not yet agreed to. Did not cover old age pension, but this was proposed later.
Philippines	All civil servants; all private sector employees (since 1960). Voluntary for self-employed below age 61 and earning P1,800 or more p/a.	11.2 million	53.2	Replacement ratios of pensions to most recent monthly salary fall from around 67 per cent for low-income earners to 52 per cent (GSIS) or 19 per cent (SSS) for high-income earners. Inflation has hurt real incomes of pensioners.

TABLE 5.11 (*Cont'd*)

Country	Beneficiaries	Number of Employees Covered	Working Population Covered (%)	Notes
Malaysia	Most of the work-force, including some self-employed persons.	2.9 million (1975) 4 million (1982)	73	Civil servants, armed forces, etc. received non-contributory pensions. Most employees contribute compulsorily through Employees Provident Fund. Lump sum or periodic withdrawals possible. Increase in value below rate of inflation.
Singapore	Virtually all the labour force.	927,000 (1982)	83	Withdrawal of balances possible after age 55. Recommended that this be raised to age 60, and that option of converting whole or part to an annuity be provided.

SOURCES: Shome and Saito (1981) and Asher (1985).

ties, home protection insurance, and shares in the Singapore
Bus Service. CPF savings will form an increasingly significant
part of reserve funds for old age as those retiring in the future
will have benefited from the high rates of contribution in recent
years. In 1983 approximately 36 per cent of Singapore citizens
aged 54 years were active CPF members. The median balance of
their savings, excluding amounts withdrawn for purchase of
flats/houses and bus company shares was $24,783. This sum
works out at a rate of $130 per month for a person living up to
70 years of age, which is the minimum household expenditure
for a single person household in 1984 based on the standard
used for calculating public assistance disbursement by the
Ministry of Community Development. Dependence on the CPF
savings alone would therefore be inadequate as inflation would
constantly raise the minimum household expenditure.

In Malaysia, the EPF contributions alone are even less likely
to provide an adequate source of retirement income, because the
level of both employer and employee contributions are less. In
Singapore, employer/employee contributions are 10/25 per cent
of employee's wages. (Until 1986, they were 25/25 per cent.) In
Malaysia, the contributions are 11/9 per cent, up from 5/5 per
cent from 1952 to 1975, and 7/6 per cent from 1975 to December
1980.

Perhaps the most surprising finding in Table 5.11 is the
relatively high percentage of the labour force covered by some
form of pension or superannuation scheme in the Philippines.
This is because not only civil servants and private employees
are covered by the Government Service Insurance System (GSIS)
or Social Service Security (SSS) schemes, but also some of the
self-employed below age 61 who earn more than P1,800 a year.
However, the pension is in many cases inadequate to provide
minimal living levels, as its ratio to the most recent monthly
salary falls from around 67 per cent for low-income earners
to 52 per cent for higher-income earners in the GSIS scheme
or 19 per cent in the private sector SSS scheme, which covers
more workers (Shome and Saito 1981, Chapter IV; Domingo 1989).
Inflation has eroded the real value of these pensions.

In Indonesia and Thailand only civil servants, employees of
state-owned enterprises, and a limited number of private sector
employees receive any kind of pension. In most cases, the bene-

fits received by these fortunate few are very substantial, raising important issues of equity. The financial support of the vast majority of the elderly in these countries depends very much on what they have been able to put aside over their working lives, what their spouse has left to them, or what support their family can provide.

ISSUES IN RETIREMENT POLICY

In the absence of national pension schemes, a retirement policy does not affect the lives of the self-employed, who still constitute the majority of workers, especially in rural areas. However, with urbanization and rapid economic development, the proportion of workers in the private sector is rising, and the official retirement policy impinges directly on their lives.

An appropriate retirement policy needs to reconcile four potentially conflicting aims:

1. To enable, although not compel, people to make the fullest contribution they can for as long as possible — not only for the benefit that comes to society from using human resources to the full, or for the benefit of employers who do not want to lose employees with valuable experience, but also for the satisfaction of the individuals concerned.

2. To make sure that people on whose capacities the changes that come with age have taken a toll do not have to continue to be employed at rates of pay that exceed the worth of work done.

3. To preserve the dignity of all concerned.

4. To ensure that arrangements are simple enough to be understood without need for professional help in interpretation.

The potential conflict between the first two aims arises from the fact that functionally, people age at different rates, so that chronological age is only roughly correlated with capacity for work; for any particular job, one person of 70 may well be functionally younger than another of 60. Mandatory retirement ages must fail to achieve either of these two aims fully. Insofar as capacities decline with age at different rates in different individuals, any fixed age will require some to retire when they still have much to give, and others at a time after they have ceased to be fully effective. The balance between these two results depends, of course, on the mandatory age chosen. Present traditional fixed ages do, however, fulfil the third and fourth aims.

There has been very little research into these issues in ASEAN countries. Table 5.5 shows a desire to work on the part of most of the elderly in Thailand. However there is little reason to doubt that among the elderly who have been working as employees in non-household enterprises, the proportion wishing to work beyond age 65 would be quite small, particularly in view of the early retirement ages that are conventional throughout the ASEAN region for such employees and which undoubtedly reflect a general attitude about the appropriate age of retirement. Aside from the desirability of a fixed (and not too high) age cut-off in smoothing the problems of dismissing older workers who are no longer wanted or needed, other reasons why governments in ASEAN countries may be reluctant to raise retirement ages are that (1) older workers are poorly educated and their replacement with younger workers raises the overall educational level of the work-force; (2) high youth unemployment may be further exacerbated if the retirement age is raised; and (3) labour market considerations would support the greater mobility engendered by the "freeing up" of jobs through early retirement.

On the other side of the coin, keeping compulsory retirement ages low may result in a loss to the economy of the potential contribution of older workers, particularly in a situation of oversupply of labour which will disadvantage older workers in looking for alternative work after retirement. It will also raise problems of financial support for retirees during the long average remaining period of their life after retirement, and is therefore closely linked with issues concerning superannuation and pension schemes addressed above.

The industrialized world provides a number of models, but certainly no consensus about appropriate retirement policies. In Japan, work-force participation by the elderly remains much higher than in countries of Europe and North America, due to policies of re-hiring workers for lower-level positions once they have reached retirement age and also because there is a gap between the age of retirement and eligibility for pensions (McCallum 1988). In the United States, compulsory retirement ages have been struck down on grounds that they violate human rights. In Australia, the trend is toward earlier retirement in a culture which emphasizes the advantages of leisure. Among ASEAN countries, Singapore's Committee on the Problems of the Aged viewed the Japanese model as one that should be emulated in keeping the elderly in the work-force longer.

CONCLUSION

Many of the elderly in ASEAN countries continue to live in the traditional rural context where an active working life shades gradually into a less active one, without the issue of "retirement" ever arising; and where the family is an economic unit which continues to support its elderly when they have ceased working. But in the cities of all the ASEAN countries, the proportion of elderly workers affected by compulsory retirement ages and having access to pensions or superannuation funds from their place of work, be it in the civil service or in the larger private firms, is undoubtedly rising. For this group of elderly workers or retirees, and for the governments involved, similar issues regarding retirement policies and social security systems are being faced as in developed countries. Given the prospective sharp increase in the share of the elderly in the total population, it is important that serious and ongoing attention be given to these issues.

6
HEALTH CARE OF
THE AGED

In high mortality populations, the aged are a very select group: they are those who have survived the dangers of being born, the risks of infancy and childhood, and the sicknesses and accidents of middle age. Until recently, in the countries of Southeast Asia, fewer than 30 per cent of those born could be expected to live to age 60.

Having survived the multiple assaults on their health during childhood and adulthood, what is the health and disability status of those increasing proportions who reach old age? Diagrammatically, the situation might be portrayed as in Figure 6.1.

The proportion of the population enjoying good health gradually declines from age 40 onwards, and the decline accelerates from about 60 onwards. Similarly, the proportion who are neither sick nor disabled declines steadily. It has been argued that, because of medical successes in postponing death but less success in reducing morbidity or disability, the gap between these curves and the mortality curve has widened in recent years, implying an increasing proportion of the elderly population who are in poor health (including an increasing proportion in poor mental health). This is, of course, related to the increasing proportion of the elderly who live to "old-old" age — beyond 75 years — implying an ageing of the aged population itself. (It was noted earlier, however, that in the ASEAN countries over the next two decades, there will not be a universal trend towards an increasing proportion of the very old among the aged population.)

FIGURE 6.1
Health and Disability Status of Those Reaching Old Age

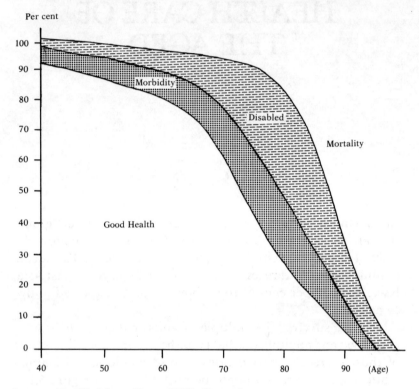

SOURCE: Modified from Myers (1985), Figure 1.

On a more positive note, Fries (1980; 1983) argues a "rectangularization of morbidity, disability, mortality" — related to a steep drop in the mortality curve around age 85, because of a postulated ultimate upper bound on life expectancy determined by biological limits on the normal life span of the human species. Fries' point is that

> the average age of onset of a significant permanent infirmity may increase more rapidly than does life expectancy, thus shortening both the proportion of life spent infirm and the absolute length of the infirm period. (Fries 1984)

Strategies for postponing infirmity include preventive approaches to premature chronic diseases, and to changes in prevalent social expectations for the elderly.

It is important to take a positive view of the increased longevity of the population. If indeed, as bodies such as the W.H.O. argue, the age of 85 is a possible outside limit of disability-free old age, the importance of promoting and maintaining health in an ageing population can hardly be over-emphasized, because during the twenty-five years of life from 60 to 85, people can make a great contribution to society.

The same general considerations apply to the mental health of the elderly. The most recent research indicates that ageing has a minimal effect on the mental functioning of healthy adults (see Garfield 1984), although the incidence of dementia does increase with advancing age among the elderly, reaching about 20 per cent among those aged over 80. These findings are significant because they contradict the stereotype of the aged person as a mentally impaired and dependent individual. They also have important implications for the appropriate retirement age.

Although, as argued earlier, increased longevity probably means that an increasing proportion of the elderly are in poor health, it is not proved that the health of the aged in developing countries is much worse than it is in developed countries. Among individuals who survive to age 60, additional life expectancy is only two years greater in developed countries. Nevertheless, a significant proportion of the elderly in all countries have significant impairment in the capacity for self-care (2 per cent among those aged 65 and over in the United States, for example) (Maddox 1982, p. 138).

EXPERIENCE AND TREATMENT OF SICKNESS

Whereas in Western countries, cancer and cardiovascular diseases cause most deaths among the elderly, the major causes of death among the elderly in the ASEAN region are infectious diseases and cardiovascular disease. In the Philippines, communicable diseases are a slightly greater cause of death than cardiovascular diseases at age 60–64, but thereafter cardiovascular diseases are more important. By age 80 and above, "others" exceed cardiovascular diseases as a cause of death, but whether this is mainly a matter of inaccurate reporting of cause of death (and the difficulty of distinguishing between the underlying and the proximate cause of death) is not clear.

Comparison of data on experience of illness or general self-evaluation of health status is very difficult because of probable differences in the definition of good health, the wording of questions used, and the reference period for experience of illness. The Indonesian population census of 1980 asked about health status; not surprisingly, with advancing age, the proportion of old people claiming to be in good health declines: from 85 per cent at age 55–59 to 80 per cent at age 60–64; 75 per cent at age 65–69; and 64 per cent at age 70+ (derived from BPS 1984, Tables 27.1, 28.1, 29.1, and 30.1).

The ASEAN Ageing Surveys collected a range of information about the health and disability status of the aged. Table 6.1 gives the percentage of respondents who claimed to have had any major illness or injury in the previous year, which affected the activities of daily living. Problems of comparability clearly arise. In Indonesia, the figures are high because the question was not restricted to the previous year. The figures are very low for Singapore, and although the elderly may actually tend to have less sickness or disability in this country than elsewhere, it is

TABLE 6.1
**Respondents Who Had Any Major Illness/Injury in the Past Year
Which Affected the Activities of Daily Living, by Sex and Age**
(In percentages)

	Indonesia*	Malaysia	Philippines	Singapore	Thailand
Males					
60–64	54	31	38	13	29
65–74	62	41	48	14	36
75+	68	37	53	18	42
All ages	61	36	45	15	35
Females					
60–64	56	57	43	9	35
65–74	58	51	48	14	38
75+	67	49	48	17	46
All ages	59	53	46	13	39
Both Sexes					
60–64	55	45	41	11	33
65–74	60	47	48	14	37
75+	68	40	50	18	44
All ages	60	45	46	14	37

* Indonesian data refer to those who *ever* experienced an injury.
SOURCE: ASEAN Ageing Surveys.

hard to accept that the figure would be only one-third as high in Singapore as in Thailand or the Philippines.

In Malaysia, the Philippines, and Thailand from one-third to almost one-half of respondents reported a significant health impairment over the previous year, the figures being higher for women than for men and increasing with age except in Malaysia.

Tables 6.2 and 6.3 give the elderly respondents' self-evaluation of their health status. There was some difficulty in matching the different categories in the different countries. Table 6.2 purports to show the proportion of respondents with quite good health, while Table 6.3 purports to show the proportion with poor or bad health. In some countries these two tables between them cover all responses; in the Philippines, Singapore, and Thailand they do not, because they used an intermediate category, "fair". The categories included in Tables 6.2 (marked *) and 6.3 (marked **) in the different countries are as follows:

Indonesia	:	Very good*	Singapore :	Very good*
		Good*		Good*
		Not too good**		Fair
		Poor**		Poor**
Malaysia	:	Very good*	Thailand :	Very good*
		Good*		Good*
		Not good**		Fair
		Poor**		Poor**
Philippines	:	Good*		
		Fair		
		Poor**		

Some of those categorized as "fair" in the Philippines and Singapore would no doubt have been categorized as "good" or "not good" if the alternative categorization scheme had been used. Inter-country comparisons should therefore not be made from Tables 6.2 and 6.3, which should be used instead for comparisons by age and marital status within countries. It should be noted, in interpreting the "both sexes" segment of the table, that the married category is predominantly males, whereas the "not married" category is predominantly females.

As expected, there is a general deterioration in reported health status with advancing age. The health status of the married is consistently better than the non-married, for both

TABLE 6.2
Respondents with Health "Very Good" or "Good" by Age, Sex, and Marital Status
(In percentages)

	Indonesia		Malaysia		Philippines		Singapore		Thailand	
	Married	Not Married	Married	Not Married	Married	Not Married	Married	Not Married	Married	Not Married
Males										
60–64	73	71	75	71	48	46	78	86	49	41
65–74	64	61	74	72	37	36	69	62	39	37
75+	46	54	72	50	41	10	60	48	29	28
All ages	65	61	74	65	42	29	71	63	41	34
Females										
60–64	76	73	64	60	37	37	70	67	37	36
65–74	67	62	70	63	44	28	70	63	31	33
75+	50	44	73	50	38	20	69	52	30	22
All ages	71	62	67	60	40	28	70	61	34	30
Both Sexes										
60–64	74	73	71	62	44	39	76	71	43	37
65–74	65	63	72	64	39	30	70	62	36	34
75+	47	46	72	54	40	17	61	52	29	23
All ages	67	62	72	61	41	28	71	61	38	31

SOURCE: ASEAN Ageing Surveys.

TABLE 6.3
Respondents with Health "Not Good", "Not Too Good", and "Poor" by Age, Sex, and Marital Status
(In percentages)

	Indonesia		Malaysia		Philippines		Singapore		Thailand	
	Married	Not Married	Married	Not Married	Married	Not Married	Married	Not Married	Married	Not Married
Males										
60–64	27	29	25	29	9	6	5	0	33	32
65–74	36	39	26	28	10	7	7	8	39	39
75+	54	46	28	50	10	22	6	13	42	51
All ages	35	39	26	35	10	12	6	7	37	42
Females										
60–64	24	27	36	40	6	7	3	1	39	39
65–74	33	38	30	37	8	14	7	3	42	41
75+	50	56	27	50	4	22	13	4	51	53
All ages	29	38	33	40	7	15	5	3	41	44
Both Sexes										
60–64	26	27	29	38	8	7	4	1	36	38
65–74	35	37	28	36	9	13	7	4	40	40
75+	53	54	28	46	8	22	7	6	44	52
All ages	33	38	28	39	8	14	6	4	39	44

SOURCE: ASEAN Ageing Surveys.

males and females. This is consistent with findings from other countries, at least as far as the working population is concerned (Lee et al. 1987). Interestingly, the differential in health status between the married and non-married tends to widen with advancing age.

Table 6.4 presents the proportions of elderly respondents who can see and hear well. A major problem with tables of this kind is whether "see well" and "hear well" are interpreted to mean without the aid of glasses or hearing aids, because this can greatly affect the proportions who say they can see or hear well. Such problems of interpretation are present in Table 6.4. For example, the proportion of the Philippines' elderly who can see well is only half that in Thailand and one-quarter that in Singapore; but this is because in Thailand and Singapore "seeing well" included those who saw well only with the aid of glasses. In Malaysia, which has a relatively low proportion who can see well, two-thirds of those with sight problems wear spectacles. "Can see well" therefore must have been interpreted as "without the use of spectacles", just as it was in the Philippines.

In Indonesia, only about 21 per cent of the elderly wear glasses; another 43 per cent need glasses but are not wearing them. Of those wearing glasses, only a quarter are able to see well, even with their glasses, suggesting that the glasses are not suitable in many cases.

TABLE 6.4
Respondents Who Can See and Hear Well by Age
(In percentages)

	Indonesia	Malaysia	Philippines	Singapore	Thailand
Can see well					
60–64	49	34	24	95	59
65–74	42	36	24	89	48
75+	28	24	18	80	36
All ages	42	33	23	89	49
Can hear well					
60–64	86	87	81	96	88
65–74	73	79	73	93	80
75+	52	73	49	82	64
All ages	74	81	71	92	79

SOURCE: ASEAN Ageing Surveys.

Of those with hearing problems in Malaysia, only 3.6 per cent use hearing aids, but 31.2 per cent expressed the need for hearing aids. In Indonesia, even fewer (0.5 per cent) wear hearing aids, although a further 26 per cent need hearing aids but do not have them.

MOBILITY AND DISABILITY

An important aspect of health status, particularly as it relates to need for assistance from others, is ability to move about. In Table 6.5 information is presented on this aspect for four of the five countries from the ASEAN Ageing Project. Although the different surveys are consistent in showing that only about 1 per cent of the elderly cannot get around the house at all (that is, they are bedridden), the interpretation of the other categories appears to differ somewhat between the different countries. For example, it seems inherently unlikely that a much lower proportion of the elderly in Thailand can get around the home without difficulty than in Indonesia. However, the data appear to be consistent in showing that more than 90 per cent of the elderly are still able to get around the house without help, a higher figure than in the West, where 70 to 80 per cent of the non-institutionalized elderly above age 65 were ambulant and needed only minimal assistance. Although, as expected, there is a steady decline in mobility with age, even among those aged 75+, more than 80 per cent in the ASEAN Ageing Surveys are able to get around the house without help.

Table 6.6 presents complementary information from Malaysia and the Philippines on the incidence of certain disabilities. This information is derived from the W.H.O. Report on health and social aspects of ageing, (Andrews et al. 1986, Chapter 5.6). It is clear that eyesight problems are among those most commonly experienced by elderly respondents. Over 60 per cent of respondents in the Philippines used glasses, and there was evidence of cataract in 57 per cent of Malaysian respondents. Dental prosthesis and difficulty in chewing were also common disabilities, experienced by more than one-third of respondents in both countries. In Indonesia, the ASEAN Ageing Surveys found an even higher proportion — 60 per cent — who had at least some difficulty chewing. The incidence of most disabilities tended to in-

Ageing in ASEAN

TABLE 6.5
Respondents by Age and
Mobility/Ability to Get Around Home
(In percentages)

	Yes, without difficulty	Yes, but with difficulty	Only with help	No, not even with help	Total
Indonesia					
60–64	93.6	4.7	1.3	0.4	100
65–74	87.9	9.1	2.4	0.6	100
75+	67.1	20.8	8.8	3.3	100
Total	86.5	9.4	3.1	1.0	100
Philippines					
60–64	80.8*				100
65–74	72.7*				100
75+	56.0*				100
Total	72.2*				100
Singapore					
60–64		94.5	5.2	0.3	100
65–74		91.8	7.7	0.5	100
75+		84.0	15.3	0.7	100
Total		91.2	8.3	0.5	100
Thailand					
60–64	74.4	24.5	0.6	0.6	100
65–74	58.4	39.8	1.5	0.8	100
75+	35	57.9	4.6	2.5	100
Total	58.7	38.3	1.9	1.1	100

* Refers to those who could get around the home without physical disability as observed by the interviewer.

NOTE: No data are available for Malaysia.

SOURCE: ASEAN Ageing Surveys.

crease with advancing age, but (unlike the findings in similar enquiries in Europe) did not differ very much between men and women.

The W.H.O. project investigated the incidence of smoking and drinking among the aged respondents. For smoking, the figures were: for males, 44 per cent (Malaysia) and 40 per cent (Philippines); for females, 19 per cent (Malaysia) and 28 per cent (Philippines). For drinking, the figures were: for males, 13 per cent (Malaysia) and 28 per cent (Philippines); for females, 7 per cent (Malaysia) and 8 per cent (Philippines).

Finally, for the Philippines and Thailand some information is presented on the incidence of a number of specific health problems. According to the ASEAN Ageing Surveys (Table 6.7) rheumatism and insomnia are clearly very common conditions, with not very much variation according to age, sex, or residence. Constipation is also quite common in Thailand but very low levels are recorded in the Philippines, suggesting differences in definitions or procedures in asking the question. High blood pressure affects more than one-tenth of the elderly in both countries. Hemorrhoids, heart trouble, diabetes, kidney problems, ulcers, and asthma appear to be fairly uncommon.

The issue of health care for the elderly is obviously a crucial one. Health care is intimately related to place of residence, and since most of the elderly live with their spouse and/or children (see Chapter 4), it is not surprising that spouse and children are the caregivers in the great majority of cases of illness among the elderly (Tables 6.8 and 6.9). Because it is much more common for elderly women to be widowed than for elderly men, a higher proportion of elderly men can rely on their spouses for care, whereas elderly women are more likely to rely on their children. Although the information is provided only for Indonesia and Thailand, it is likely that the situation does not differ very much in the other ASEAN countries.

TABLE 6.6

Persons Suffering from Certain Disabilities by Age Group and Sex, Malaysia and the Philippines
(In percentages)

| Disability/Country | Male | | | | Female | | | | Both Sexes |
	60–64	65–74	75+	Total Male	60–64	65–74	75+	Total Female	Total
Hearing problems									
Malaysia	14	15	31	18	n.a.	n.a.	n.a.	n.a.	n.a.
Philippines	15	19	43	25	16	24	46	25	24
Sight problems									
Malaysia	44	69	81	65	59	71	73	68	67
Philippines	75	80	81	79	85	80	81	82	81
Evidence of cataract									
Malaysia	51	60	67	59	40	62	56	54	57
Philippines	18	18	37	21	12	24	33	21	22
Dental prosthesis									
Malaysia	25	31	32	30	46	45	39	44	37
Philippines	30	40	47	38	49	47	46	48	43

TABLE 6.6 (*Cont'd*)

Disability/Country	Male				Female				Both Sexes
	60–64	65–74	75+	Total Male	60–64	65–74	75+	Total Female	Total
Difficulty chewing									
Malaysia	36	54	55	50	37	46	61	46	48
Philippines	24	32	51	33	24	39	33	33	33
Foot problem restricting activity*									
Malaysia	6	3	9	5	8	9	18	11	8
Philippines	3	1	3	2	6	4	4	4	3
Difficulty walking 300 metres									
Malaysia	8	8	30	12	12	14	35	17	15
Philippines	9	24	44	23	17	31	51	30	27

n.a. — Not available.

* Bunions, corns, bent toes, long toe nails, varicose veins, etc.

NOTE: Number of females with hearing disabilities for Malaysia in the original data used in the compilation of this table are internally inconsistent and have been excluded.

SOURCE: Computed from Gary R. Andrews et al. (1986, Tables 19, 24–26).

TABLE 6.7
**Respondents Suffering from Specific Health Problems,
the Philippines and Thailand**
(In percentages)

	Total	Age			Sex		Residence	
		60–64	65–74	75 +	Male	Female	Urban	Rural
Philippines								
Rheumatism	18.5	20.0	14.5	24.8	20.5	16.9	18.0	18.8
High blood pressure	13.2	12.2	13.1	15.0	11.9	14.5	22.9	6.9
Heart problem	7.4	7.9	7.8	6.0	5.6	8.9	15.5	1.9
Kidney problem	3.3	4.2	1.8	5.3	5.6	1.5	4.1	2.8
Lung problem	2.3	4.2	1.4	1.5	3.7	1.2	5.3	0.6
Asthma	3.8	4.2	4.2	2.2	3.7	3.8	4.9	2.5
Ulcers	4.1	5.3	3.5	3.8	4.5	3.8	4.9	3.6
Constipation	1.5	2.6	1.4	0	1.5	1.5	0.8	1.7
Thailand								
Rheumatism	74.6	73.7	73.7	77.8	71.0	77.0	70.0	75.5
Constipation	39.9	37.5	39.3	44.8	39.1	40.4	42.3	39.4
Bloody stools (hemorrhoids)	10.1	10.5	10.0	9.9	13.6	7.7	12.5	9.7
Insomnia	58.8	58.3	58.4	60.2	53.8	62.2	50.9	60.4
Heart problem	7.5	7.8	7.8	6.4	6.1	8.5	10.9	6.8
Diabetes	2.3	2.5	2.6	1.2	2.2	2.3	6.1	1.4
High blood pressure	11.6	11.5	11.6	11.5	10.5	12.3	18.0	10.1

SOURCE: ASEAN Ageing Surveys.

TABLE 6.8

Who Takes Care of the Elderly When They Are Ill by Residence and Sex, Indonesia

(In percentages)

	No Illness	Spouse	Children/ In-Laws	Nephew/Niece/ Other Cousins	Friend/ Neighbour/ Others	Nobody Takes Care	Total %	N
Urban								
Male	3.1	62.9	29.4	3.1	1.3	0.2	100	615
Female	3.5	16.1	59.5	16.3	3.7	0.8	100	632
Total	3.3	39.2	44.6	9.8	2.6	0.5	100	1,247
Rural								
Male	2.9	50.3	40.4	4.3	1.8	0.3	100	1,069
Female	3.5	10.5	67.3	15.2	3.5	0.2	100	1,214
Total	3.2	29.2	54.6	10.1	2.7	0.2	100	2,283

SOURCE: ASEAN Ageing Surveys.

TABLE 6.9

Who Takes Care of the Elderly When They Are Ill by Age, Sex, and Residence, Thailand

(In percentages)

	No Illness	Spouse	Children	In-Laws	Nephew/ Niece	Other Cousins	Friend/ Neighbour	Others	Nobody Takes Care	Total %	N
All Respondents	6.2	18.7	62.1	1.3	5.9	1.3	0.6	0.7	3.2	100	3,221
Age											
60–64	7.3	25.0	58.4	0.7	3.0	1.5	0.7	0.6	2.8	100	1,047
65–74	6.1	17.8	63.0	1.4	5.1	1.4	0.6	0.6	4.1	100	1,458
75+	4.7	10.7	66.1	2.3	12.4	0.8	0.2	0.7	2.0	100	689
Sex											
Male	7.6	34.4	48.2	0.6	3.4	0.9	0.5	0.8	3.5	100	1,321
Female	5.2	7.8	71.8	1.9	7.7	1.6	0.6	0.6	3.0	100	1,899
Residence											
Urban	9.2	19.5	48.8	1.2	9.7	2.4	0.9	1.8	6.6	100	553
Rural	5.6	18.5	64.9	1.4	5.2	1.1	0.5	0.4	2.5	100	2,667

SOURCE: ASEAN Ageing Surveys.

7
SERVICES PROVIDED AT NATIONAL AND LOCAL LEVELS

ASEAN countries, whether of necessity or from philosophical conviction, seek to maintain the existing system of family care and concern for the elderly. The family is seen as ultimately responsible for its elderly dependants, and institutionalization to be used only as a last resort. The aim is to obtain as much community participation as possible. This philosophy is reflected in the kinds of income maintenance, health care, recreational programmes, and publicly funded institutional care available to the elderly. Governments provide limited special services for particular groups of the aged, and rely on private and charitable groups to assist in providing for the needy. Social security programmes are typically limited to employed individuals with complementary special welfare programmes for the impoverished and the impaired.

Thailand is perhaps typical of the other ASEAN countries in the increasing attention given in government development plans and in welfare programmes to the needs of the aged (see Debavalya and Boonyakesanond 1982). The Thai Government set up the National Committee on Ageing in February 1982, chaired by the Minister of the Interior. This committee has established seven subcommittees and held a national "Seminar on Roles of all Organisations in Longterm Planning for Elderly Population". In the Fifth Five-Year Plan (1982–86), the needy aged are considered a special target group along with many other underprivileged groups such as orphans, needy children, victims of disasters, the disabled, etc. In addition, it is the policy of the government to encourage the participation of the private sector in the provision of social welfare services for the needy aged. The plan aims to strengthen the family as a basic social unit to enable it to care for its own elderly members more adequately. As well as residential care where needed, non-institutional care, particularly in the form of social service centres for the elderly, will be expanded. In terms of health care, the under-5s and over 60s are singled out as groups to receive special emphasis. A programme of free medical care for those aged over 60 is being gradually introduced in general hospitals throughout the country.

HEALTH SERVICES

"No known system of geriatric care is optimal in the sense that demonstrably effective comprehensive care is achieved at low cost" (Maddox 1982, p. 147). There is therefore scope for individual nations to develop health care systems for the aged that are responsive to prevailing traditions and values. There is a danger, however, that in planning health care systems in ASEAN countries, the heavy emphasis in development planning on human resource development will lead to an emphasis on health care for the young and those of working age. Stronger concentration on the elderly would require an emphasis

> either on ethical and humane considerations or on the perception that the youngest persons among the elderly can be assisted through adequate health care to remain socially productive for an additional number of years. (Maddox 1982, p. 148)

In recent years, the emphases among those planning health care systems throughout the world has been increasingly influenced by W.H.O.'s call for primary health care systems that are cost-effective in emphasizing preventive health care to alleviate the burden of ill-health that can only be dealt with inadequately (and expensively) by health care systems emphasizing hospital-based curative services.

In the developed nations, planning of health care in recent times has emphasized four universal themes: cost containment; assurance of equitable access to appropriate care; development of appropriate manpower; and increased involvement of informed consumers in taking responsibility for their own care. The same themes are clearly of major concern, as well, in developing countries. Budgetary constraints are especially important in developing countries, which are therefore faced with the dilemma that cost containment is likely to be achieved at the expense of quality, access, or both. For this reason, developing countries also have a strong incentive to explore the potential and limits of individual and family involvement in the promotion and maintenance of health.

With regard to the aged, the same general points can be made. Although hospitals, and the medical personnel and technology concentrated in them, will continue to play a vital role in geriatric care, the experience of the developed nations shows that heavy investments in physical plant, sophisticated technology, and highly specialized training should not be undertaken as a matter of course. An effective system of health care will be one that is responsive to a nation's cultural traditions, seeks to involve individuals and communities in programmes of health education and promotion and prevention of sickness, and seeks to maximize the informal support and services to the aged from kin and neighbours.

The elderly account for a much higher proportion of hospital admissions than their proportion of the population (for example, 18 and 8 per cent, respectively, in Singapore in 1985). If the proportion of elderly spending time in hospitals or living in nursing homes is to be held down, both preventive health care and provision of assistance to family caregivers will need to be emphasized. A Singapore study on the health care needs of the elderly living in the community (Singapore 1987) found that help with bladder and bowel functions was needed by 38 per cent of the respondents. The actual types of assistance required included bed change for the incontinent, help with bedpan for the non-ambulant, and help to the toilet for the frail and semi-ambulant. Another 24 per cent required assistance with bathing and 17 per cent assistance with moving about. Physical rehabilitation and turning in bed are required by 18 and 8 per cent respectively. These needs put a heavy burden on family caregivers, and show the need for the development of home nursing services or other means of lessening the burden of care imposed by the frail elderly without the need to institutionalize them.

A variety of measures have already been taken in ASEAN countries aimed at preparing for the rapidly growing number of old people. For example, in Thailand, the Ministry of Public Health has set up health care units for the aged in seventeen general hospitals outside Bangkok and in seven hospitals in Bangkok, and plans to set up geriatric clinics in both government and private hospitals all over the country. In the Philippines, the few geriatric clinics are mostly in the urban areas. In Singapore, medical services for the aged are believed to be adequate at present. But to meet future needs, modifications in the distribution of health care services and facilities are needed, as well as the establishment of a department of geriatrics to provide specialized care for the aged and to train medical and paramedical personnel to manage the aged sick. Based on present hospital admission rates among the aged in Singapore, the number of hospital admissions is expected to more than double between 1982 and the year 2000, and the aged would account for almost 30 per cent of all admissions by that time.

Perhaps the greatest need at this stage is for preventive health at the middle ages, to avoid some of the health problems typically faced in old age. Given the rapid economic growth in the ASEAN countries, attention must be given to the health problems of affluence as well as those of poverty.

FINANCIAL SUPPORT SERVICES

As mentioned earlier in this book, there is no general system of old age pensions in any ASEAN country. Moreover, the proportion of the elderly population covered by superannuation or pension schemes organized by their former employers, either government or large firms, ranges downward from 36 per cent in Singapore (of those aged 54 years), to 8 per cent in the Philippines (of all old people), and lower still in Thailand and Indonesia. Government assistance programmes are oriented specifically to particular groups of needy persons. For example, in Singapore the Ministry of Community Development provided direct financial assistance to 2,850 persons, representing about 1.6 per cent of all aged persons. In addition, various voluntary and charitable organizations give aid on a regular or *ad hoc* basis. Current rates of public assistance per person are pegged at 69 per cent of the minimum household expenditure as determined by the Statistics Department of the Ministry of Trade and Industry. The prevailing government policy is to be as stringent as possible in the selection of recipients and in the amount given, both in order to maintain the incentive for people to take up gainful employment and to encourage family members to provide financial support for their aged.[1]

In Thailand, employees of government and state enterprises and large-scale private firms are entitled to receive welfare services of one kind or another, but those who were self-employed or worked for small firms generally are not. Direct government financial support for the aged is given only in rare instances of special need. The *wat*, or Buddhist temple, may also serve as a support mechanism for aged persons who enter the monkhood. In Malaysia, the welfare department gives financial support (M$30 to M$50 per month) to limited numbers of destitute old people (about 7,000 or 1.4 per cent of the aged population), and supplies free spectacles for the very poor elderly. Similarly, in the Philippines financial support is given only to limited numbers in particular need.

In the Philippines, around 8 per cent of the total aged population receives pensions from the Social Security System (SSS) if they were employed in the private sector, from the Government Service Insurance System (GSIS) if they were government employees at the time of retirement, or from the Veteran Affairs Office if they were veterans. In 1978, the SSS had 55,000 pensioners on its books, each receiving an average of US$24 a month or US$293 a year. In 1980, the GSIS was giving retirement benefits to 40,000 government retirees an average of US$41 a month or US$491 a year. Considering that the average income of a Filipino family in 1975 was around US$597 (for six persons), the GSIS and SSS pensions are a significant addition to the family income.

HOME CARE SERVICES

In Singapore, the Home Nursing Foundation (HNF) was established in 1976 with the following purposes:

a. provide nursing care for the disabled and non-ambulant sick in their own homes;

b. encourage and promote community interest and participation in the care of the aged sick; and

c. co-operate with other relevant public and private agencies in providing home nursing.

The HNF is a joint effort of the government and the community. The salaries of the nurses and administrative staff are paid by the government while the day-to-day expenses for medicines, food supplements, surgical materials, and equipment are met from public donations. In its publicity, the HNF stresses that the physical and moral support the elderly receive in familiar surroundings helps keep them mentally alert and creative and hastens their physical recovery (HNF 1983/84).

A complementary policy in Singapore is provision of income tax relief of S$1,000 to a taxpayer for supporting each of the aged parents/grandparents staying with them.

In Thailand, eight elderly social service centres have been established in different parts of the country, and more are in the planning stage. These centres provide services to the elderly in nearby areas, including heads of households who face problems with the elderly under their responsibility. Services provided in these centres are therapeutic and rehabilitative care, recreation, day care, family assistance, and counselling services. Home visits are also made in surrounding communities to give advice and primary medical treatment to elderly persons. One aim of these centres is to enable the elderly to remain with and be taken care of by their families, thus reducing the need for additional homes for the aged.

RECREATIONAL SUPPORT

As the Report of the Committee on the Problems of the Aged in Singapore noted, the mental and physical well-being of elderly persons depends greatly on how well they spend their time: maintaining interest in work, keeping up existing social contacts, and pursuing new interests and activities. Government and private services can assist them in this.

In the Philippines, Senior Citizens' Clubs have become favourite media for the elderly to interact with peers, articulate their needs, express interests, and participate in volunteer work. There are 247 clubs established all over the country by non-government organizations. In Thailand, 36 Senior Citizen Clubs have been established in 36 provinces, providing health, religious, and recreational services. Other associations are formed by persons retired from the same organization or profession, such as the Retired Interior Officials Association, Retired Military Association, etc. In Singapore, there are 163 Senior Citizens Club (66 of them provided by the People's Association, 77 by Residents' Committees, 14 by Citizens' Consultative Committees, and 6 by voluntary organizations). It is estimated that 8 per cent of Singapore's aged population are members. Most are managed by volunteers and function mainly in the afternoons, weekends, or at night. In Indonesia, 24 per cent of the elderly belong to old people's organizations, 20 per cent participate in educational programmes for the elderly, and 16 per cent are involved in PK3A (BPS 1984).

ADEQUACY OF SERVICES

We do not have enough information at this stage to evaluate the services and social policies relating to the aged in each ASEAN country. Such evaluation would be very difficult, even if better information were available, because although the elderly have specific physical and financial needs that must be met, their overall well-being is dependent as well on their effective integration into the community in a way that leaves them with a feeling of dignity and usefulness.

There is general agreement that old age homes are impossibly expensive, as well as unsatisfactory in many other ways, as a solution to the living problems of the aged in ASEAN countries. Their role should be to cater to the small proportion of elderly who have no other options available to them. But planning is required to maximize the number of elderly who do, in fact, have other options available to them. Given the increasing urbanization of the ASEAN region, coupled with falling birth rates and rising levels of women's participation in the work-force, one of the key areas for government assistance appears to be in helping families and neighbours to care for the aged who live alone or in family groups.

It would appear, however, that much more needs to be done in the ASEAN countries to provide assistance of this kind to urban families. Day care centres, home nursing services, meals on wheels, and befrienders' services are all being provided to a limited extent in cities by both government and voluntary agencies. And in rural areas — where most of the elderly in ASEAN countries still live — the elderly and their families are very much "on their own". The needs of the rural aged need to be identified, as well as the kinds of services by government and private agencies that could realistically be provided in rural areas to meet their needs. Besides this, evaluative programme research is needed of possible aids to families attempting to cope with caring for disabled elderly members. Services such as short-stay homes, day care, night care, live-in home aides to provide families some respite and vacation, and specific professional nursing interventions need to be evaluated as to their impact on the family, perhaps through pilot projects.

As far as financial support for the elderly is concerned, as urbanization increases and more people are employed in government and large firms, consideration needs to be given to the most effective kinds of superannuation and pension schemes. In Singapore and Malaysia, CPF schemes provide a lump sum payment on retirement. Although this does not involve the government in problems of maintaining annual payments as life expectancy increases, it also means that if the lump sum payment is squandered, the old person loses the chance of securing regular income after retirement. Consideration should be given to the possibility of the retiree using part or all of the CPF balance to purchase an annuity. There are various mechanisms through which this could be achieved, including the involvement of private sector financial institutions in converting the lump sum into an annuity.

The example of the Philippines (and of Sri Lanka, see Jones 1988, Table 8) indicates that it is not necessary for a country to reach high per capita income levels before developing quite comprehensive provident fund schemes covering the employed population and some of the self-employed as well. This could be kept in mind in Thailand and Indonesia as they seek to develop more comprehensive schemes than those presently in effect.

Notes

1. Some further financial relief for the aged is provided in Singapore through income tax concessions for earned income, concession fares on public transport and recreational parks, and concessions at government out-patient dispensaries.

8
ROLE AND CONTRIBUTION OF THE AGED IN THE COMMUNITY

Given the increasing length of life after retirement from work, it is important that the potential contribution of the elderly in the community be maximized, and that they be treated as a resource rather than a burden. In Western countries, efforts are increasingly being made to tap the abilities and interests of the aged through such programmes as retired executives' programmes in which retired executives provide voluntary assistance in the running and management of small businesses; foster grandparents' programmes in which elderly people can become surrogate grandparents to children or young people who lack close family or are estranged from close family for some reason; and involvement in a wide range of community activities and associations requiring the input of time, of which the elderly have more to spare than do younger people who are in the work-force or busy raising families.

In Southeast Asia, there is less "institutionalization" of the community role of old people, but because of the respect accorded to age, and the prevalence of community activities involving all age groups rather than age group-based activities characteristic of more highly urbanized societies, there is a more automatic involvement of the elderly in the affairs of the family and of the community. For example, in the Philippine survey, about 40 per cent of the elderly females reported that they spent most of their time caring for other family members.

Related to the role of the elderly in the community is the question of their leisure time activities. It is clear from Table 8.1 that listening to the radio and watching TV are important leisure time activities, being engaged in by roughly half the respondents in all countries, with little difference between the sexes. Talking with friends/neighbours occupies about a quarter of respondents in most countries, though fewer in Singapore and much more in Thailand. The importance of reading appears to differ quite markedly by country and sex, the differentials being linked, no doubt, to differentials in literacy. In view of the low level of literacy among the elderly in the region, the TV and radio, with their capacity to entertain and educate without the need for literacy, must be seen as a tremendous boon to the elderly.

Unfortunately, the structure of the questions on which Table 8.1 is based does not permit a very clear picture about the importance of handicrafts among the elderly, because knitting, crocheting, and needlework were combined with reading. However, in the Philippines, where handicrafts were listed separately, around one-third of both males and females stated that they participated in handicraft activities.

TABLE 8.1
Respondents Engaging in Various Leisure Time Activities
(In percentages)

Activities	Indonesia		Malaysia		Philippines		Singapore		Thailand	
	Males	Females	Males	Females	Males	Females	Males	Females	Males	Females
Talking with friends/neighbours	12	12	21	22	28	17	15	12	90	86
Knitting/Reading/Crocheting/Needlework	12	7	1	7	23[a]	16[a]	17	5	53[c]	17[c]
Gardening	n.a.	n.a.	14	12	n.a.	n.a.	2	2	64	44
Listening to the radio	11	5	22	22	43	43	7	3	73	62
Watching TV/video	10	6	27	28	3[b]	1[b]	45	52	67	58
Games/Sports/Recreation	4	2	15	10	38	32	14	26	4	2
Handicrafts	n.a.	n.a.	n.a.	n.a.	0	0	n.a.	n.a.	c	c
Others	49	68	0	0	0	0	0	0	0	0

[a] For the Philippines, only includes "reading".

[b] For the Philippines, only includes "sports".

[c] "Rattan weaving" was included with "reading".

n.a. — Not available.

9
POLICY IMPLICATIONS AND RECOMMENDATIONS

It was stressed in the early part of this report that ageing is a gradual process, and that by the end of the century (fifteen years from now) only Singapore and the non-Malay population of Malaysia will be reaching levels of ageing comparable to those of the least aged Western countries today. The other ASEAN countries will be ageing only gradually, although the absolute numbers of aged will be increasing very rapidly and their ageing process will accelerate in the early decades of the twenty-first century.

Ageing, therefore, should not be considered an unmanageable process, particularly in view of the fact that overall dependency ratios will be falling in ASEAN countries, even though the aged dependency ratio will be increasing. A positive emphasis on harnessing the potential of old people to assist in development and community welfare is more appropriate than stressing the burdens imposed by an ageing population.

It cannot be denied, however, that ageing takes on some problematic dimensions in the context of social and economic trends in the region. The most basic dilemma is to decide, in a context of scarce resources and government dedication to the goal of raising rates of economic growth in the interests of the community as a whole, how many resources should be devoted to a group who cannot be viewed as human capital for development, as their working and childrearing life has largely ended.

The most worrisome problems facing the elderly in the region appear to be ill health and financial difficulties, with loneliness a problem faced by many. These are the problems, then, that public policy must seek to address.

Cultural preference as well as budgetary limitations in most ASEAN countries ensure that care of the elderly (both financial and material) will be left largely in the hands of families. Though comprehensive social security policy for the elderly would be desirable,

> in social security, as in many other areas of social policy, action depends not only on what is socially desirable but also on what is financially possible and administratively feasible. (ILO 1982, p. 3)

But a continued reliance on family support as the proportion of the aged population rises could put great stress on family members. The burden would fall heavily on women, who usually are the primary caregivers, and on impoverished families, who have no resources to spare. In any case, increased urbanization and social mobility, smaller families, and the tendency for married women to be in the paid work-force, all suggest the possibility that parents will not be able so readily to assume that their children will care for them in their old age. A key need, then, is to increase options for the equitable and effective support of the dependent aged through traditional family support, government interventions, and combinations of the two.

Patterns of population mobility can also cause problems in the care of the aged. In some rural areas, exodus of young adults to the cities leaves distorted age and sex structures among those left behind, and although remittances are normally sent back to remaining family members, questions remain about the care which the elderly left behind in the villages can expect.

In urban areas, housing is expensive and typically designed with the nuclear family (and a fairly small one at that) in mind. Public housing policies need to take cognizance of the need to encourage three- and four- generation households in some cases, or alternatively the need for elderly persons and their children to live close to each other. Public policy also needs to consider seriously the kinds of support needed by the elderly living alone, or by families caring for elderly members, if the alternative of more old age homes is to be avoided.

The composition of the elderly population and its changing characteristics need to be monitored carefully in planning for effective provision of services. As noted earlier, the high proportion of widows among the elderly should be borne in mind in designing support programmes. Similarly, the low literacy rate of the elderly highlights the value of the radio and TV in their entertainment. Over time, however, literacy levels of the elderly will be rising, and reading can then play a more important role in their leisure time activities. Because of the prevalence of sight problems among the elderly, programmes of making books available in large type may then become justifiable.

Voluntary and charitable agencies play an important role in caring for the aged in the ASEAN region. Governments can foster such activities by highlighting the needs of the aged in information campaigns, and in giving appropriate financial and other support to voluntary agencies to enable their efforts to achieve greater results.

As noted in Chapter 5, there are many complex issues related to the work patterns and income maintenance of the aged. There are arguments for keeping retirement ages relatively low, and counter-arguments for raising them. Similarly, a wide range of income maintenance schemes for the elderly are found in Western countries, and a range of philosophies about the role of the state in income maintenance. Within the ASEAN countries themselves, the approaches to income maintenance for the elderly differ widely, but the emphasis has been on compulsory income contributory schemes for those in the public sector and larger private firms rather than on taxation-based pension schemes to provide an income "floor" for the entire elderly population. The latter are seen as too burdensome to government budgets in relatively low-income countries. Thus, responsibility for a large proportion of the elderly continues to be passed on to families. But with changes in the social and economic setting, as well as a steady rise in the proportion of elderly in the population, it is not yet certain that families will be able to bear this responsibility.

With the steady rise expected throughout the region in the proportion of workers employed in the civil service or in larger private firms, continuing attention needs to be given to appropriate superannuation or employees provident fund schemes to ensure that a growing proportion of all workers will have a measure of income security when they leave the work-force. Closely related to this, compulsory retirement ages for civil servants and private sector employees are very low in Indonesia,

Malaysia, Singapore, and Thailand. With lengthening life expectancy and improving health conditions, consideration will certainly need to be given to raising these retirement ages.

In Chapter 2, it was emphasized that the proportion of the aged in Malaysia, Thailand, and Indonesia will double in less than forty years and in Singapore, in an even shorter period. By the 2030s, the proportion of the aged will be rising very rapidly indeed in countries such as Thailand and Indonesia. This will put great strains on traditional family mechanisms, and could lead to a break in the continuity of inter-generational exchange, leading to a degree of neglect in old age of a generation which had already played its part by actions in mid-life to support ageing parents. Moreover, unless these old people are covered by an effective superannuation scheme, the burden of providing a taxation-based income support scheme for them may be too great for the shrinking proportion of working-age persons to bear. So although the 2030s may seem a long way off, action is needed now to develop an effective employees provident scheme, because those who will be elderly in the 2030s are already in the work-force today.

Finally, one perhaps controversial point might be made. In terms of government policy, there is more scope for effective intervention in issues of ageing that arise in respect of the urban population, even though the rural aged (like the rural population as a whole) are poorer and in this respect therefore more in need of assistance. In rural areas, the tendency to remain in the work-force until physical incapacity prevents it, the high proportion who are self-employed or unpaid family workers, the close-knit family support mechanisms, and the less concentrated population (making provision of some kinds of public facilities impracticable) means that at this stage, there is little scope for (or, in one sense, need for) government programmes specifically directed to the aged in these areas. If this point is accepted, then only about one-third of the elderly population in the ASEAN region can be offered much by way of government programmes at this stage. A specifically urban focus in planning for the aged may assist in defining in clearer terms what government programmes for the aged can expect to accomplish. However, on equity grounds, it is important that the rural aged be assisted, and appropriate ways to do this need to be investigated.

Appendix
SAMPLING DESIGN USED IN COUNTRY SURVEYS

Except in Singapore and Thailand, where national representative samples of randomly selected elderly living in the community were conducted, the surveys were designed to capture a broad cross-section of the elderly in different geographic areas and social and economic strata, rather than to be statistically representative of the entire country. The cost of achieving statistical representativeness was considered to be too great in Malaysia, the Philippines, and Indonesia, and in any case these surveys were considered a pioneering effort designed to obtain a broad picture of the circumstances of the aged and to open up issues for further research.

The following is a discussion of the details of the survey designs adopted in each country. Appendix Table A.1 presents the total number of households and elderly respondents interviewed.

APPENDIX TABLE A.1
Total Number of Households and Elderly Respondents Interviewed

Country	Sample
Indonesia	4,500 households, each with a respondent aged 55 or more (400 with a respondent aged 60 or more).
Malaysia	3,000 households, which yielded 1,254 respondents aged 55 and more.
Philippines	1,321 individuals aged 60 or more.
Singapore	1,013 elderly living in the community.
Thailand	3,246 elderly, derived from approximately 100,000 households.

INDONESIA

The survey was integrated with the Inter-Censal Population Survey (SUPAS) of 1985, conducted by the Central Bureau of Statistics, the households chosen for interview being a subset of those covered in the SUPAS. The survey was confined to Java, which contains just over 60 per cent of Indonesia's population. Interviewing was conducted in July–August 1986 by thirty-two qualified enumerators, mostly graduates of the Academy of Statistics.

Households were selected from strata chosen to give adequate representation to major economic activities. The strata were municipalities/urban districts, and rural districts with main activities in agriculture, fishery, manufacturing industries, and trade. Two municipalities/regencies were selected from each stratum. A sample of 800 households was chosen from each stratum, or 400 households from each municipality/regency. This made a total of 4,000 households with at least one member aged 60 and over.

The areas selected were:

1. Municipalities: Bandung (West Java) and Banyumas (Central Java).
2. Regencies with strong representation of activities in the following:
   a) Agriculture   : Garut (West Java) and Banyumas;
   b) Fishery   : Pasuruan (East Java) and Brebes;
   c) Manufacturing : Sidoardjo (East Java) and Kudus (Central Java); and
   d) Trade   : Tasikmalaya (East Java) and Jember (East Java).

MALAYSIA

The sampling was conducted by the Department of Statistics using its available census listings. The sample was restricted to three west coast states — Selangor, Negeri Sembilan, and Melaka. Within these three states, stratified by urban and rural residence and ethnicity, systematic random sampling was used. A sample size of 2,000 respondents was originally aimed for, but was later reduced to 1,500 because of budget constraints. All districts within the three chosen states were included in the sample, and from these districts blocks were selected randomly. A total of 3,912 living quarters was selected randomly from these blocks, yielding 985 households with eligible respondents. As many of these had more than 1 eligible respondent. A total of 1,254 respondents was interviewed: 46 per cent males and 54 per cent females. By ethnicity, 48 per cent of respondents were Malays, 34 per cent Chinese, 17 per cent Indians, and less than 1 per cent others. Field-work was conducted in March–April 1986.

PHILIPPINES

The nation was first stratified into regions where each of the three main language groups (Ilocano, Tagalog, and Cebuano) predominated. Within each region, areas showing high proportions in the 60 and over age category were then identified. Based on these criteria, the following three provinces were selected: Ilocos Norte (Ilocano), Batangas (Tagalog), and Bohol (Cebuano). In addition, an urban sample was drawn from Metro Manila, again selecting concentrations of the three language groups. In Metro Manila, the following barangays were selected: Barangay 163, 164, 165 in Tondo (Tagalog areas); Barangay Sto. Niño in Quezon City (Ilocano); and Barangay Bagong Lipunan ng Crame, Barangay Kaunlaran, and Barangay Martin de Porres in Quezon City (Visayan).

Because this survey was conducted in collaboration with another project which required the study of population communication between the elderly and married women and adolescents, slightly more than half the respondents in each region were selected on the basis of households having at least one married woman of reproductive age or one adolescent present, whereas this was not a requirement in selecting the remaining respondents. This may have had some effect on the family structure of the sample as a whole.

The numbers of elderly interviewed by region (a total of 1,321) were as follows: Ilocos Norte (220); Batangas (220); Bohol (221); and Metro Manila (660). Since the urban sample constituted half the total sample, this means that urban respondents are over-represented (compared to the proportion of the nation's aged living in urban areas) in tables where urban and rural areas are combined.

SINGAPORE

The main survey, whose findings are presented in the comparative tables in this report, was a national representative sample of 1,013 randomly selected elderly (aged 60+). The field-work was conducted in November 1986. In addition to this survey, two other surveys were conducted. The first was among the elderly living in institutions providing residential care for the aged and aged sick in Singapore. The second was a survey of the elderly sick in the community, conducted among two groups of elderly: those who were treated as out-patients and those warded in government and private hospitals.

THAILAND

Thailand conducted a nationally representative household survey, covering about 10,000 households which yielded a total of 3,246 elderly respondents. In addition, 2,111 persons aged 15–44 were interviewed to determine their attitudes towards the elderly and the process of growing old. The survey was conducted in March–May 1986.

PROBLEMS ENCOUNTERED

No major difficulties were encountered in the conduct of the surveys, although there were some problems with regard to estimating the number of households needed to yield the required number of elderly respondents. In some countries (for example, Malaysia) this required an increase in sample size over the original estimates. The main problems in the field-work related to difficulties some elderly respondents had in answering the questions. In general, elderly respondents experienced greater difficulty in understanding the questions, in remembering past events, and in some cases even in hearing the interviewer, than would be the case with a sample of younger respondents. Therefore the average interview took longer to complete than would be the case with younger respondents, and in some cases this exhausted the respondents.

REFERENCES

Adi Rianto. "A Case Study of the Homes for the Aged in Jakarta". In Social Research Center (1982).

Andrews, Gary et al. "Cross-national Study of Social and Health Aspects of Aging — Korea, Malaysia, Philippines and Fiji". Paper presented to the XIIIth International Congress of Gerontology, New York, 1985.

Andrews, Gary R., Adrian J. Esterman, Annette J. Braunack-Mayer, and Cam M. Rungie. *Aging in the Western Pacific*. Manila: World Health Organization, Regional Office for the Western Pacific, 1986.

Aries, Philippe. *Centuries of Childhood*. London: Jonathan Cape, 1973.

Asher, Mukul G. "Forced Saving to Finance Merit Goods: An Economic Analysis of the Central Provident Fund of Singapore". Occasional Paper 36. Canberra: Centre for Research on Federal Financial Relations, Australian National University, 1985.

Bergener, M., M. Ermini, and H.B. Stahelin. *Dimensions in Aging*. London: Academic Press, 1986.

Binstock, Robert H., Wing-Sun Chow, and James H. Schultz, eds. *International Perspective on Ageing: Population and Policy Challenges*. Policy Development Studies No. 7. New York: United Nations Fund for Population Activities, 1982.

Biro Pusat Statistik (BPS). *Penelitian Tentang Masalah Kesejahteraan Sosial Lanjut Usia 1982/83* [Study of social welfare problems of the aged 1982/1983]. Jakarta: BPS, 1984.

Bulatao, Rodolfo A. *On the Nature of the Transition in the Value of Children*. Papers of the East-West Population Institute, No. 60-A. Honolulu: East-West Population Institute, 1979.

Cain, Mead. "The Consequences of Reproductive Failure: Dependence, Mobility, and Mortality Among the Elderly of Rural South Asia". *Population Studies* 40, no. 3 (1986).

Chan Kok Eng. "Socio-Economic Implications of Population Ageing in a Developing Country: the Malaysian case". In International Association of Gerontology, Asia/Oceania Region, *Proceedings of the 2nd Regional Congress*. Singapore, January 1983.

Chaudhury, Rafiqul Huda. "The Aged in Bangladesh". In Social Research Center (1982).

Chen Ai Ju and Paul P.L. Cheung. *The Elderly in Singapore*. Phase III ASEAN Population Project. Socio-Economic Consequences of the Ageing of the Population, Singapore Country Report. Singapore, 1988.

Cherlin, Andrew J. and Frank F. Furstenberg, Jr. *The New American Grandparent: A Place in the Family, A Life Apart*. New York: Basic Books, 1986.

Clark, Robert L. and Joseph J. Spengler. *The Economics of Individual and Population Aging*. Cambridge, Mass.: Cambridge University Press, 1980.

Coale, Ansley J. "The Effects of Changes in Fertility and Mortality on Age Composition". *Milbank Memorial Fund Quarterly* 34 (1956): 79–114.

Cowgill, Donald O. "Aging and Modernization: A Revision of the Theory". In *Late Life: Communities and Environmental Policy*, edited by J.F. Gubrium. Springfield, Ill.: Charles C. Thomas, 1974.

Cowgill, Donald O. and Lowell D. Holmes. "The Demography of Ageing". In *The Daily Needs and Interests of Older People*, edited by Adeline M. Hoffman. Springfield, Ill.: Charles C. Thomas, 1970.

———, eds. *Ageing and Modernization.* New York: Appleton-Century-Crofts, 1972.

Debavalya, Nibhon and Visit Boonyakesanond. "Role of Older People in the Development in Thailand and Its Policy Implications". Paper presented at the International Symposium on Ageing Society: Strategies for the 21st Century, Tokyo, 1982.

Domingo, Lita. "The Filipino Elderly: Issues and Policy Implications". Paper prepared for the project "Interrelationships of Population, Human Resources, Development and the Philippine Future", Center for Integrative, and Development Studies, University of the Philippines, Quezon City, Philippines, May 1989.

Economic and Social Commission for Asia and the Pacific (ESCAP). "Report of a Regional Survey of the Ageing". Paper presented at the Technical Meeting on Ageing for the Asian and Pacific Region, Bangkok, 27–30 January 1981.

Fries, James F. "Ageing, Natural Health and the Compression of Morbidity". *New England Journal of Medicine* 303 (1980): 130–35.

———. "The Compression of Morbidity". *Milbank Memorial Fund Quarterly* 61 (1983): 397–419.

———. "The Compression of Morbidity: Miscellaneous Comments about a Theme". *The Gerontologist* 24, no. 4 (1984).

Fries, James F. and Lawrence M. Crapo. *Vitality and Aging: Implications of the Rectangular Curve.* San Francisco: W.H. Freeman, 1981.

Garfield, Eugene. "Social Gerontology. Part I. Ageing and intelligence". *Current Contents* 14 (2 April 1984): 3–13.

Giele, Janet Zollinger. "Family and Social Networks". In Binstock et al. (1982).

Hauser, Philip M. "Ageing of Population and Labour Force for World, More Developed and Less Developed Areas and Their Regions: Population Ageing 1970–2025; Labour Force Ageing

1970–2000". *NUPRI Research Paper Series No. 15*. Tokyo: Nihon University Population Research Institute, 1983.

Hetler, Carol B. "Female-Headed Households in a Circular Migration Village in Central Java, Indonesia". Ph.D. thesis, Department of Demography, Australian National University, Canberra, 1986.

International Labour Organization. "Income Maintenance and Social Protection of the Elder Person: Income Security for the Elderly". Paper presented at the World Assembly on Aging, Vienna, 1982.

Inkeles, Alex and David H. Smith. *Becoming Modern: Individual Change in Six Developing Countries*. Cambridge, Mass.: Harvard University Press, 1974.

Jones, Gavin W. "Implications of Declining Fertility for Old Age Security in Asia". Paper presented at the International Union for the Scientific Study of Population (IUSSP) seminar on "Fertility Transition in Asia: Diversity and Change", Bangkok, 28–31 March 1988.

Keyfitz, N. "Indonesia's Future Population". Jakarta, 1985. Mimeographed.

Kuroda, Toshio and Philip M. Hauser. "Ageing of the Population of Japan and Its Policy Implications". *NUPRI Research Paper Series No. 1*. Tokyo: Nihon University Population Research Institute, 1981.

Lee, Sun-Hee, Len Smith, E. D'Espaignet, and Neil Thompson. "Health Differentials for Working-Age Australians". Canberra: Canberra Highland Press, 1987.

McCallum, John. "Japanese *Teinen Taishoku*: Evidence for Macro-Social Factors in Retirement". *Aging and Society* 8, no. 1 (1988).

Maddox, George L. "Challenges for Health Policy and Planning". In Binstock et al. (1982).

Maeda, Daisaku. "Ageing in Eastern Society". In *The Social Challenge of Ageing*, edited by D. Hobman. New York: St. Martin's Press, 1978.

Myers, George C. "Mortality and Health Dynamics at Older Ages". Working Paper No. 73, Ageing and the Family Project. Research School of Social Sciences, Australian National University, Canberra, 1985.

————. "The Ageing of Populations". In Binstock et al. (1982).

Naim, Mochtar. "Report on the Present and Potential Impact of the Ageing Population Structures on Selected Social and Economic Institutions. The Asia and Pacific Region: An Indonesian Case". Vienna: UNIDO, 1981.

Napaporn Chayovan and Malinee Wongsith. "The Problem of the Elderly in Thailand, Preliminary Analysis" (in Thai). Paper presented at the Thai Population Association Conference, Bangkok, 26–27 November 1987.

Notestein, Frank W. *Proceedings of the American Philosophical Society, No. 98.* 1954.

Nugent, Jeffrey B. "The Old-age Security Motive for Having Children". *Population and Development Review* 11, no. 1 (1985).

Petri, Peter A. "Income, Employment and Retirement Policies". In Binstock et al. (1982).

Preston, Samuel H. "Children and the Elderly: Divergent Paths for America's Dependants". *Demography* 21, no. 4 (1984).

Shome, Parthasarati and Kathrine Anderson Saito. *Social Security Institutions and Capital Creation: Singapore, the Philippines, Malaysia, India and Sri Lanka.* Kuala Lumpur: Meta, 1981.

Singapore, Ministry of Labour. *Labour Force Survey.* Ministry of Labour, 1983.

Singapore, Home Nursing Foundation (HNF). *Annual Report 1983/84.* Singapore, 1984.

Singapore, Ministry of Health. *Report of the Committee on the Problems of the Aged.* Singapore: HNF, 1984.

————. "Survey on the Aged and Aged Sick Living in Institutions". Singapore, 1986.

Singapore, Ministry of Social Affairs. *Report on the National Survey of Senior Citizens*. Singapore: HNF, 1983.

Singh, Gurmukh. "The Future of Gerontology in Malaysia". In International Association of Gerontology, Asia/Oceania Region, *Proceedings of 2nd Regional Congress*. Singapore, January 1983.

Social Research Center, University of Santo Tomas. *The Elderly of Asia*. Manila: Unitas Publications, 1982.

Strange, Heather. "The Effects of Modernization on Rural Malay Aged — A Pilot Study". *Social Welfare Journal* 1, no. 2 (1980).

Sunarto. "The Economic Livelihood of the Aged in the Special Region of Jogjakarta" (in Indonesian). *Cakrawala* (Universiti Kristen Satya Wacana) 10, no. 6 (1978).

Treas, J. and B. Logue. "Economic Development and the Older Population". *Population and Development Review* 12, no. 4 (1986): 645–73.

United Nations (U.N.). *The Ageing of Population and Its Economic and Social Implications*. Population Studies No. 26. New York, 1956.

_____. *Report of the Secretary General to the World Assembly on Aging, Vienna, 26 July–6 August 1982*. New York, 1982.

_____. *Report of the World Assembly on Aging, Vienna, 26 July–6 August 1982*. New York, 1982.

_____. *Demographic Yearbook*. Various years.

U.N. Department of International Economic and Social Affairs. *Global Estimates and Projections of Population by Sex and Age: The 1984 Assessment*. New York, U.N., 1987.

Welford, A.T. "Retirement: Gerontological Considerations for Policy Making". In Bergener et al.

White, Benjamin. "Production and Reproduction in a Javanese Village". Ph.D. thesis, Department of Anthropology, Columbia University, New York, 1976.

Wong, Aline and Eddie Kuo. "The Urban Kinship Network in Singapore". In *The Contemporary Family in Singapore*, edited by Aline K. Wong and Eddie C.Y. Kuo. Singapore: Singapore University Press, 1979.

THE EDITORS

DR CHEN AI JU, Deputy Director of Medical Services for the Primary Health Division, Ministry of Health, Singapore, is the Regional Project Co-ordinator for the project "Socio-Economic Consequences of the Ageing of the Population" of the Phase III ASEAN Population Programme. She is active in health services research and studies on the epidemiology of ageing and chronic degenerative diseases. She has been closely associated with the Singapore population programme and its policies and is presently in charge of the Population Planning Unit in the Ministry of Health.

DR GAVIN W. JONES is Professorial Fellow and Acting Head of the Department of Demography, Research School of Social Sciences, at the Australian National University. His academic writings focus on issues in the determinants and consequences of demographic trends in Asia, particularly Southeast Asia. He has served as consultant to planning agencies in Thailand, Malaysia, Indonesia, and Sri Lanka and has taught in universities in Indonesia and Malaysia. His recent publications include *Women in the Urban and Industrial Workforce: Southeast and East Asia* (1984), *The Demographic Dimension in Indonesian Development* (co-authored with Graeme Hugo, Terence Hull, and Valerie Hull) (1987), and *Urbanization and Urban Policies in Pacific Asia* (co-edited with Roland Fuchs and Ernesto Pernia) (1987).